How to
Apply
the Bible

How to Apply the Bible

DAVE VEERMAN

This Billy Graham Evangelistic Association
special edition is published with permission
from Tyndale House Publishers.

Tyndale House Publishers, Inc.
Wheaton, Illinois

This book was published with the assistance of The Livingstone Corporation.

Library of Congress Cataloging-in-Publication Data

Veerman, David.
  How to apply the Bible / David R. Veerman.
    p. cm.
    ISBN 0-913367-60-5
    1. Bible—Use. I. Title.
  BS538.3.V44 1993
  220.6—dc20   92-40732

Printed in the United States of America

*To Gail
My best friend
and life partner,
my love*

*Thanks also to
Dr. Bruce Barton
and
Dr. James Galvin,
my friends and
partners in ministry
and business,
who developed
much of the
material in
this book.*

CONTENTS

APPENDIXES

PART ONE
Preparing for Applications

CHAPTER ONE
Why Apply?

● "Let's get going, everyone, or we'll be late!" Bill calls up the stairs. "I'll get the car warmed up." After a couple of impatient honks of the car horn, Joanne, Billy, Sarah, and Todd pile into the minivan. Quickly Bill backs out of the drive and heads for church. He has to be there early this Sunday to interview new members . . . and then there's choir . . . and worship . . . and Sunday school (he and Joanne teach the junior high class). Bill and his family are immersed in church activities. Bill is a leader there— confident, capable, spiritual, and available—everybody knows they can count on him.

But Bill's not so sure. Inside he carries self-doubts and worries about the future that he hasn't shared with anyone, not even Joanne. The pressure has been building at the office, and Bill is afraid that he'll be the next to be let go. He may be a success at church, but he feels like a failure at work.

● After hearing a dynamic tape on the importance of studying God's Word, Sally was determined to have a daily quiet time. So she sets her daily alarm at 6 A.M. and reads for a half hour before getting dressed. So far, she's only missed two days in six weeks (she was sick). Gwen, her roommate, has really been impressed with Sally's discipline and "spirituality," and she has said so on several occasions.

Sally wonders, however, if she's doing something wrong. The

daily readings are beginning to feel like drudgery . . . work. She just doesn't seem to connect with Scripture. And she sure doesn't feel very spiritual the rest of the day.

● Ruth is known for her contagious smile and warm words. She seems to be on a first-name basis with everyone in the neighborhood and church. People often compliment Ruth on her gifts of hospitality and encouragement. "How can she always be so 'up'?" one friend commented.

While Ruth is succeeding "out there," she really struggles at home. Constant bickering with a teenage daughter and arguments with her husband leave her frustrated and discouraged.

● An honor student and varsity basketball player, Tim is the picture of the all-American boy. He is also an active member of the church youth group and a Christian club on campus, and he is very serious about his faith. Tim has grown up in the church and knows all the Christian vocabulary.

But Tim wants to know how to bring what has been taught in church and what he believes about Christianity into his everyday life. At school it seems as if he is bombarded by questions about popularity, sex, the future, and morality. On Sundays, Tim sits in the back of the church and wonders.

Do you recognize any of those people? Although you may have never met Bill, Sally, Ruth, or Tim, you probably know many just like them. Or maybe you recognize yourself in one of the descriptions. These men and women are typical Christians—they are what our churches are made of—needy people, some desperate, looking for help.

Where can they find the truth about life? Where can they find guidance and direction for how to act at work, home, and school? Where can they find comfort in time of need? For Christians, the answer is obvious, almost too obvious—it has been repeated from pulpits, in Sunday services and classes, and in evangelical literature for centuries—*in the Bible.*

After all, the Bible is God's Word, and "whatever God says to us is full of living power: it is sharper than the sharpest dagger, cutting swift and deep into our innermost thoughts and desires with all their parts, exposing us for what we really are" (Hebrews 4:12).

God gave his Word to us through the Bible writers—"For no prophecy recorded in Scripture was ever thought up by the prophet himself. It was the Holy Spirit within these godly men who gave them true messages from God" (2 Peter 1:20-21).

So, "the whole Bible was given to us by inspiration from God and is useful to teach us what is true and to make us realize what is wrong in our lives; it straightens us out and helps us do what is right. It is God's way of making us well prepared at every point, fully equipped to do good to everyone" (2 Timothy 3:16-17).

Clearly, then, the Bible *is* the answer. Through the years, millions of people have realized that fact and have made the Bible the best-selling book in history. And many people own several Bibles.

Unfortunately, the overwhelming number of people who own Bibles don't read them much. According to research by the Barna Research Group,* 93 percent of all the households in America own one or more Bibles. But of this group, 57 percent do not read the Bible at all during a typical week. The number one reason given for not reading the Bible is the perception of irrelevance. In other words, most people, even those who own Bibles, don't believe that the Bible has anything to say about today, their society, and their lives. "After all," they reason, "the Bible was written hundreds (some books, thousands) of years ago, to a land and culture thousands of miles away. The Bible is an ancient book. What can it possibly have to say to me?" So they don't even crack the covers.

Of course, *reading* is just the *first,* most basic, step. Next, the Bible must be understood. Let's say that someone decides that the Bible does, in fact, have a message for today. Here we encounter another perceived barrier—31 percent of *all* adults in America say that the Bible is too difficult to understand. Perhaps they remember seeing as a child the huge, old, dusty family Bible on Grandma's cof-

*George Barna, *The Frog in the Kettle* (Glendale, Calif.: Regal Books, 1990)

fee table—it was mysterious . . . and heavy. They may remember hearing a minister reading the King James Version from the pulpit, and they didn't know what many of the words meant. Maybe they tried reading the Bible themselves and stumbled over the *thees, thous,* and *wouldests* or got lost trying to find Obadiah. They may even have tried to understand Scripture by using Bible reference books, but the tiny print just explained facts—words such as *wormwood, Septuagint, Pentateuch,* and *Ammonites*—when they wanted to know about worry, stress, peer pressure, and anger. Whatever the barrier, many obstacles keep these motivated people from *understanding.*

Others, like Bill, Sally, Ruth, and Tim, read the Bible and understand much of what it is saying. But, as we have seen, for these folks something still is missing. There's a gap between the Scripture they read and the lives they live.

I grew up in a very strong evangelical church. We believed in the inerrancy and infallibility of Scripture. In Sunday school I sang, "The B-I-B-L-E, yes, that's the book for me; I stand alone on the Word of God, the B-I-B-L-E." Each summer I went to DVBS (Daily Vacation *Bible* School). Each spring, I memorized verses to earn my way to church camp. I competed in Bible quizzes. And over the years, I heard a steady stream of sermons from God's Word. Certainly I was convinced of the inspiration of Scripture, and as much as possible, I was a student of the Word. I knew a lot *about* the Bible and a lot *in* the Bible. I read and understood God's Word. But something was missing for me as well. I found it easy to relegate the Bible to the "spiritual" area of my life—my Sunday and church world. But rarely did the truth of the Bible touch the rest of my world—school, friends, work, even family.

James wrote about this kind of problem: "And remember, it is a message to obey, not just to listen to. So don't fool yourselves. For if a person just listens and doesn't obey, he is like a man looking at his face in a mirror; as soon as he walks away, he can't see himself anymore or remember what he looks like. But if anyone keeps looking steadily into God's law for free men, he will not only remember it but he will do what it says, and God will greatly bless him in everything he does" (James 1:22-25). According to James, then, we are to *do* what the Bible says, not just read and understand it.

In commenting on the purpose of the Old Testament Scriptures, Paul wrote: "All these things happened to them as examples—as object lessons to us—to warn us against doing the same things; they were written down so that we could read about them and learn from them in these last days as the world nears its end" (1 Corinthians 10:11). Paul was saying that reading the Bible should affect the way we live.

And listen to what the prophet Isaiah told God's people: "Won't even one of you apply these lessons from the past and see the ruin that awaits you up ahead?" (Isaiah 42:23).

It is clear from James, Paul, and Isaiah that we are supposed to be *doers* of God's Word and not just *hearers* of it. But how can we tell how well we are applying the Bible? Consider the following five steps in the application process:

BIBLE →	1	2	3	4	5	→ LIFE
	READ	UNDERSTAND	COMPREHEND	APPLY	DO	

1. READ—open the Bible and read a passage; get a general idea of the story
2. UNDERSTAND—know what all the words mean; learn the facts; see the concepts
3. COMPREHEND—find the biblical principles, the timeless truths that God wants to communicate
4. APPLY—see myself in the story and how the biblical principles relate to my life; make the timeless truths timely; see what God wants me to do
5. DO—design an action plan; obey God and put into practice *now* what he has taught me in his Word

These steps are necessary to bring the Bible to life. Each step is important; action that isn't based on God's Word may be misdirected, wasted, or even harmful. On the other hand, merely reading the Bible is of some profit, but it misses the purpose for which it was written. Step 1, reading, is the bare minimum. Step 5, doing, is the goal. Consider where you would place yourself on these steps. Which word most closely describes your relationship with Scripture? Where do you tend to get stuck?

The key step between the Bible and life is *apply*. That's where the truths of Scripture begin to move beyond statements of fact or principles. Simply defined, *apply* means putting knowledge to practical and specific use. So biblical application means allowing the truth of Scripture to penetrate our lives, to make a difference in how we live.

We need to apply God's Word . . .

Because of who God is: God knows us and he knows everything about us, our talents, potential, gifts, fears, and foibles. No one knows us better than God. Not only that, God loves us and wants the very best for us. It only makes sense to discover God's will—and we will settle for less than the best without it.

Because of who we are: We are finite and fallible . . . and sinful. We can't see the future, we don't know ourselves very well, and we easily forget the past. Left to our own devices, we stumble, fall, and fail. We need help. We need direction. We need wisdom. We need encouragement. We need answers.

Because of the way the world is: Our world is fallen, filled with sin and sinful people and ruled by Satan. It is filled with temptations, questions, pressures, and pitfalls. God doesn't want to remove us from the world; he wants to use us to make a difference in the world (John 17:13-18). God wants to work in us and through us to reach others.

Simply put, we need to know what God wants us to do, and then we need to do it!

This book will help you understand God's Word and then show you how you can apply it to your life. In the course of our study, we will remove some barriers, explode some misconceptions, and explain clearly what Bible application is. Then we will discover two Bible study methods. In one we'll climb a Pyramid, and in the other we'll look through a Window. The ultimate goal is to give you the tools to dig into God's Word, mine for applications, and bring the treasure home—in short, to help you bring the Bible to your life.

In the next chapter we will take a closer look at *application.*

WORKING IT THROUGH

Take a moment to assess your relationship with God's Word. Circle the number that is most appropriate for each step.

1. READ—I can read a passage in the Bible and get a general idea of the story. In *reading* the Bible, I am:

1—bad   2—poor   3—all right   4—good   5—very good

I think I can improve my Bible reading skill by:

_____

_____

_____

2. UNDERSTAND—When I read the Bible, I can figure out what the words mean, learn the facts, and see the concepts. In *understanding* the Bible, I am:

1—bad   2—poor   3—all right   4—good   5—very good

I can probably improve my Bible understanding by:

_____

_____

_____

3. COMPREHEND—As I study the Bible, I can find biblical principles, the timeless truths that God is trying to communicate. In *comprehending* the timeless truths of the Bible, my skill level is:

1—bad   2—poor   3—all right   4—good   5—very good

My Bible comprehension probably could be improved by:

_____

_____

_____

4. APPLY—When I read and study the Bible, I can see myself in the story; I can see how the biblical principles relate to my life, and I can see what God wants me to do. My skill in *applying* Bible truths to my life is:

1—bad   2—poor   3—all right   4—good   5—very good

I think I can improve my application skills by:

_____

_____

_____

5. DO—Based on my study of the Bible, I can design an action plan to obey God and put into practice *now* what he has taught me in his Word. In *doing* what I learn from God's Word, I am:

1—bad   2—poor   3—all right   4—good   5—very good

I'm pretty sure that I could improve my doing skills by:

_____

_____

_____

6. I need to apply God's Word to my life because . . .

_____

_____

_____

Chapter at a Glance

To bring the Bible to life I must:
  ● Read ● Understand ● Comprehend ● Apply ● Do
I need to apply God's Word:
  ● Because of who God is
  ● Because of who I am
  ● Because of the way the world is

CHAPTER TWO

What Is Application?

Little Johnny loved bicycles. He would search through magazines for the pictures of men and women riding their ten-speeds on scenic bike paths, faces awash with sun. During the Olympics he sat transfixed, watching every cycling race. As he grew older, Johnny began to read about bicycles: first in the *B* volume of his family encyclopedia and then in books from the library. Soon he knew the history of the modern bicycle, all the different kinds, and how they were made. Of course Johnny saved his money and eventually bought a wonderful bike. He put it in a special place in the garage and made sure it was safe and shiny. Johnny loved bicycles . . . and he never lost that love and interest. Later, as an adult, John joined a bicycle club—at many of the meetings, men and women would share their cycling experiences, about the thrill of riding and their various adventures.

One fresh, spring day, sitting in his office high above the city, John looked down at the bike path along the lake and again saw cyclists riding slowly along the shore, weaving around the walkers and joggers. Turning from the window, he picked up the model ten-speed from his desk and fingered it thoughtfully. "I wonder," he mused, "if I'll ever learn to ride."

That apocryphal story may seem a bit farfetched. After all, how could anyone profess to love bicycles and not ever ride one? That would be like a fisherman never fishing, a pilot never flying, or a cellist never playing.

But that's how many Christians treat the Bible. They profess to love God's Word. They may even study it and memorize it. In fact, they could pass a Bible literacy test with ease. And they have attended countless meetings where others have testified about changed lives. But if these Bible students were honest, they would admit that they seldom, if ever, have put what they have learned and what they have memorized into practice. Their Bible knowledge has made very little difference in their lives.

This problem is not limited to individual believers. Consider the weekly Bible study group that ends with the leader saying something like: "Now don't forget to put what we've learned into practice." Then after closing prayer and refreshments, the studiers file out and back into their daily routines.

Or what about Sunday's biblical fare? My friend once explained that the best thing she could ever say about her pastor's sermons was, "That was interesting," or "I never knew that before." She longed for the *Wow!* factor, when she would feel blessed, motivated, and challenged.

It's the missing ingredient in many Bible studies, sermons, and Christian lives: *application.*

WHAT APPLICATION IS

Very simply stated, application is answering the question "So what?" Another, perhaps more gentle, way of stating that would be: Why should I know these facts? How can I use this information? What am I going to do about what I have just learned? What should I do about it?

- "I know a lot about bicycles."
  So what?
- "I know how to tie a fly for trout fishing."
  So what?
- "I know John 3:16 by heart."
  So what?

● "Love is very patient and kind, never jealous or envious, never
boastful or proud, never haughty or selfish or rude" (1 Corinthians
13:4-5).

    So what?

Application focuses the truth of God's Word to specific, life-related
situations. It helps people understand what to do or how to use what
they have learned. Application persuades people to act.

That's a short definition and summary. Before we get into this
much further, however, we should look at what some people substitute for application. These days the word *application* is used quite
often in Christian publishing—check out the dust jackets of the most
recent study Bibles on the market, the covers of the latest Bible
study materials, and the promotional material for church curricula.
Almost everyone is *for* application. In fact, just about every Bible
study guide will have at least a line or two with that label. And every
pastor and Bible teacher I know will admit that application is
extremely important. But as politicians have taught us, just saying so
doesn't make it so. And we know from interpersonal communication
that words can have different meanings to different people.

Here are some Bible study steps and sermon points that often pass
for application.

WHAT APPLICATION ISN'T

1. *Information.* This is simply getting the facts. Whether in detective
work (a la Sgt. Friday: "Just the facts, ma'am.") or in Bible study,
gathering facts is an important first step, but it is not enough. We still
need to know how to use those facts. It is good to know that Matthew was a tax-collector and to learn how tax-collectors worked for
the Roman government and usually became rich at the expense of
their countrymen. This information helps put Matthew in context and
helps us understand the Bible. But it is just the first step.

2. *Concepts.* This is deeper than fact-collecting and is also an important step in studying the Bible. We need to know what the Bible
means, not just what it says. *Understanding* follows *Reading* in the

Bible study process. Again, however, this is not the same as application. Many people understand biblical truths without changing their lives. You may understand that Jesus quoted Scripture to counter Satan's attacks in the wilderness and that the Word of God is powerful, but "So what?" What does that mean for you? James explains: "Are there still some among you who hold that 'only believing' is enough? Believing in one God? Well, remember that the demons believe this too—so strongly that they tremble in terror!" (James 2:19). Satan has a good understanding of the Bible.

3. *Relevance.* This step explains how what happened in Bible times can happen today. For example, when we learn that Corinth was a lot like cities today—a wild city, filled with false religion and sexual immorality—we will be more open to application. When we see that what happened many centuries ago is similar to what is happening today, we will understand that the truths from 1 Corinthians are, in fact, timeless. They are for all people, including us. But this step also falls short of application—it doesn't tell us what we can do about those biblical principles.

4. *Illustrations.* This means seeing how someone else handled a similar situation. Illustrations can shed light on the meaning of a passage and can show us how someone else applied a timeless truth to his or her life, as is the case with personal testimonials. But it is still removed from the individual . . . from you and me. When explaining "peacemakers" in Matthew 5:9, NIV, a story about an international peacemaker will enlighten our Bible study group, but it will not show us where or how we can and should make peace.

If that's what application *isn't,* then what steps will lead a person to applying the Bible? We will cover these in depth in Parts Two and Three (that's what this book is all about). But, in brief and in general, here are the steps.

STEPS TO PERSONAL APPLICATION
1. *The person (reader or listener) must receive the message.* This step sounds easy, but often the process stops right here because the

receiver is not open to hearing God's Word. Some people simply go through the motions with their minds distracted as they sit in church or read the Bible. Remember when you wished the pastor would finish before noon because you had dinner in the oven, or when your mind wandered to thoughts about sports, finances, or family matters during the Bible class? At those times, we aren't very receptive to God's message.

Others have blocked communication with God through disobedience or secret sin—they may look as if they are getting it, but they really don't want to hear what God is telling them. I worked with high school students for many years. Usually I could spot when an individual was struggling in his or her Christian life (often in the area of sex and dating). The student would avoid me on campus because he or she felt guilty. That person knew what he or she was doing was wrong but wanted to do it anyway. Seeing me was a reminder of God's disapproval, and the student really didn't want to listen to God right then.

Reception can also be hindered through poor communication by writers, preachers, and teachers who twist the message, get lost in minutiae, or make it boring. Of course, the speaker may be engaging and entertaining but not really get to the point. That also may block communication. After hearing one such speech, I remember thinking, "That was great!" But if someone had asked me, "What did he say? What was the point?" I wouldn't have had an answer.

This first step to personal application of the Bible means *being open to God as he speaks through his Word*. It means approaching Scripture (and sermons and lessons) with the prayer, "Lord, speak to me," and eagerly anticipating God's direction, counsel, and personal communication.

2. *The person should reflect on his or her life.* This is simply *putting the Bible truths and principles into a personal context*, asking, "What does the message mean for me?" In other words, it means looking at Bible study from a personal perspective, going beyond the historical and cultural context, the words in the text, and the theology. It also means taking a look, an honest look, at our lives, antici-

pating that there will be a lesson to learn and apply. For example, as I read Ezekiel, I need to imagine myself in that story and put the prophet and God's message into mine. "What am I going through that is similar to what I am reading?" "What would God say to me if Ezekiel came to my house with God's message?"

This second step means "taking it personally," consciously looking for application areas.

3. *The person should identify what he or she needs to change.* This step is really an extension of the previous one. After asking, "What area of my life does this speak to?" we should ask, "What should I do about it?" This means being action oriented—ready and willing to obey God in those areas where the Holy Spirit is convicting. Let's look at each of the words in that important question:

WHAT—looking for a specific action to take
SHOULD—understanding that the message is to be obeyed
I—recognizing that the application is for me; not "What should *he* (or she or they) do?"
DO—seeing that action, obedience, is involved
ABOUT—knowing that the action is a response . . .
IT— . . . to a biblical teaching

The answer to "What should I do about it?" may be, "Nothing at this point, but have you considered . . . ?" In essence, this third step looks for an answer to "So what?"

4. *The person should lay out a plan to make that change.* The question to answer here is, What should I do right away? This involves thinking through the application and laying out a plan of action. It means answering the question "Now what?" Now that I know what God wants me to do, what am I going to do about it? Where am I going to start? What will be my first step?

Suppose that in reading 1 Corinthians 13, I am convicted about my relationship with my wife, Gail. In answering "So what?" I decide that I need to be more loving to Gail, especially when she has had a rough day. That's good, but it's incomplete because I still need to answer "Now what?" In other words, how will I do that? What will be my first step in putting that truth into practice in my life? I need a plan.

The fourth step means actually *doing* what God has told us to do. We will discuss this in depth in chapter 10.

So far, we have discussed why application is important, what application is *not* and what application *is,* taking a broad look at the steps involved. Actually, it seems pretty simple, doesn't it? So why is application so difficult? That's our next consideration.

WORKING IT THROUGH

1. How has your idea of "application" changed through reading this chapter?

_____

_____

_____

2. In one sentence, how would you explain what it means to apply the Bible?

_____

_____

_____

3. In what areas of your life do you feel a pressing need to allow God to work?

_____

_____

_____

4. What passage of Scripture has been most meaningful to you recently? Why?

_____

_____

_____

5. How would you describe the difference between "So what?" and "Now what?"

_____

_____

_____

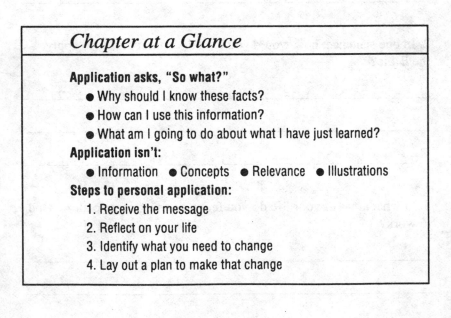

Chapter at a Glance

Application asks, "So what?"
- Why should I know these facts?
- How can I use this information?
- What am I going to do about what I have just learned?

Application isn't:
- Information ● Concepts ● Relevance ● Illustrations

Steps to personal application:
1. Receive the message
2. Reflect on your life
3. Identify what you need to change
4. Lay out a plan to make that change

CHAPTER THREE

Why Is Application So Difficult?

● "Apply, apply, apply!"

With this strong challenge echoing in her mind, Sharon picks up her Bible with renewed determination. At a retreat two months ago, she trusted Christ as Savior. Filled with the excitement of her new-found faith, Sharon had devoured all of the literature she was given. The booklets had been very helpful. Then she had tried to read the Bible on her own, beginning at the beginning. Genesis was fascinating, and Exodus was pretty interesting. But she had been stopped cold by all the laws, rules, and instructions in Leviticus. Switching to the New Testament, Sharon was slowed down by the genealogies in Matthew. But this time she hopes things will be different.

Sharon wants to read, understand, and apply Scripture, but she can't figure out how.

● "All right, everyone, let's get started!"

The small clusters of animated discussions settle to whispers and then die out as everyone turns toward the Bible study leader. For the next several minutes, Robert explains the background of the passage and shares his insights gleaned from selected commentaries. Then he asks the group what they have learned from their personal study in preparation for the lesson. After a few comments, an eternal moment of embarrassing silence engulfs the room. Then Robert concludes with a few thoughts on the importance of these verses and of obeying God.

Robert was trying to lead a Bible study, but he left feeling defeated—the group just didn't connect with the text.

● "Desperate" is an apt description for Marie. A twenty-five-year-old sales representative with three young children, she is trying to juggle the incredible demands of work and single-parenting. Marie is a Christian and very serious about her faith. She wants to do what God wants in every area of her life, especially with her children. Church attendance and regular Bible reading are important parts of her schedule, but they don't seem to translate into action plans.

How does obedience to Christ make a difference with these screaming kids?! she wonders.

Most Christians *want* to apply the Bible, and most Bible preachers and teachers want to preach and teach toward application. Despite their desires, however, it doesn't seem to be happening. The spirit is willing, but the applications are weak. In many cases, the bottom line is that we don't know what to do.

REASONS FOR WEAK APPLICATIONS

1. *Hard work.* Perhaps the main cause of weak applications (or no applications at all) is the fact that they are hard work and take time. It can also be quite threatening to look honestly at our lives in light of Scripture because it may require a change that we don't want to make.

I had the privilege of being a senior editor for the *Life Application Bible.* As the editorial team discussed this enormous project, we decided that our goal was to help the reader ask the right questions and then motivate him or her to action. That was our definition of "application" for the notes.

As I began my work, I thought that I would have little trouble writing application notes. After all, I had ministered for two decades with young people, challenging them to follow Christ and teaching them how to grow in their faith. But it turned out to be tough work. I did find it interesting and enjoyable to research and then explain textual questions, cultural influences, and theological intricacies, but I couldn't make the bridge to real life. Even now, after years of writing application notes for study Bibles and Bible studies, I find that seeing applications in the text doesn't come easy. And it's even more difficult to think through applications for myself. But it is vital!

2. *Wrong assumptions.* Another cause for the absence of application is that many preachers and teachers assume that the congregation, class, or study group will make the connection between the lesson and their lives by themselves. This is a common assumption. Not wishing to insult the intelligence of their listeners, they lay out the Bible story, the theological insights, or the timeless truths and leave the rest to the audience to figure out (like the pastor I knew who would end sermons with, "And you?"). But most people can't make the mental jump—they don't have that innate ability. Believers don't have to be spoon-fed, but they do need to be led.

The same is true for personal Bible study. Many Christians treat the Bible as though it were a magic book. They think that if they simply read a passage, the meaning and application will jump out at them—God will speak to them each time they open his Word. That's possible, of course; God can do anything he wants. But he has given us a mind to use. That's why he wants us to *study* the Bible (see 2 Timothy 2:15).

A few years ago, my pastor was preaching a series of sermons on Hebrews. The texts and titles for the messages were listed in the bulletin so that the congregation could be prepared. Because I was helping plan the worship services that month, I called Pastor Mike early in the week to talk over the next Sunday's service. I wanted to know what songs and readings to include.

"What direction are you going with the sermon?" I asked.

"Well, you know from the bulletin insert that the topic is 'Jesus is greater than the angels,'" Mike answered.

"I mean, what do you want us, the congregation, to do as a result of the sermon? How do you want us to respond?"

I went on to joke with Mike that if his objective was to convince us that Jesus is superior to angels, we'd believe him just because he told us—that in fact, because that statement was already in the bulletin, we wouldn't even have to stay for his sermon!

I must interject that making applications is one of Mike's strengths. In our phone conversation, he quickly admitted he had been working hard to make the passage relevant and hadn't thought of application yet.

3. *Fear.* Another reason for weak applications, by pastors and teachers especially, is the fear of being too simplistic. They may think that they have to be deep or complex to properly proclaim the Word of God. Or maybe subconsciously they are trying to prove that they learned something in seminary. Too often ministers preach to themselves, splitting the finer points of theology, extrapolating the etymology, or considering the cultural context, while the congregation waits for a life-changing challenge.

I've worked hours crafting sermons that I delivered with confidence, only to have everyone stare back with a collective "ho hum." It's not that I wasn't prepared or pre-prayered, or that I stumbled or stuttered. In fact, the congregation probably learned something, and after the sermon quite a few people would say, "Thank you," "That was interesting," "Good job." But nothing was said about changed lives. I had failed to move to application.

When moving out of state, I preached a farewell sermon in the church I attended in Louisiana. I was almost embarrassed with the basic message and simple outline. But the response was overwhelming. As the people left church that Sunday, one by one they told me what they were going to *do* as a result of God speaking to them. Although the sermon was not complex, it was practical, touching people where they lived.

The same principle applies to personal Bible study. Sometimes people think they have to find the "deep truths" or hidden meanings in the passage. But the timeless truths and personal applications are often quite simple.

4. *Poor preparation.* Many sermons and lessons are weak on application because the applications have not been thought through ahead of

time. The pastor or teacher may have extensive notes, yet just a word or two jotted down for application. Perhaps the speaker is trusting the Holy Spirit to give him the right words when he gets to that point in the message; or maybe he wants to be flexible and go the direction that seems right at the time. Whatever the reason, the applications often seem tacked on or inappropriate.

For personal Bible study, this problem is merely a matter of not leaving enough time for taking the application steps. Surrounded by study helps, we may do everything we can to understand the passage, investigating the cultural and historical context and checking out all the unknowns. But it would be far better to take a smaller passage of Scripture and have time for application.

5. *No training.* Another reason for weak applications is the lack of seminary training in Bible application. I've spoken to many pastors who bemoan this gap in their education. While being grateful for the intensive work in biblical languages, theology, church history, and so forth, they express their need for a dose of reality. "I wish I had been taught how to relate the Word to the needs of real people," said one.

Pastors who haven't been trained in how to apply the Bible will find it difficult to train others.

6. *Wrong idea.* Finally, applications can be weak because of a misunderstanding of what application is. We covered those wrong ideas in chapter 2 under "What Application Isn't." The person who is unsure of his or her goal will have trouble hitting it.

MISCONCEPTIONS ABOUT APPLICATION

Some people oppose all this talk about application. But I find that their opposition is based on one or more misconceptions. These voices of opposition may be characterized by the following statements.

1. *"The Christian life cannot be reduced to a set of formulas."* This statement assumes that application means giving people an easy-to-use, easy-to-follow set of instructions to solve a problem, resolve a conflict, and so forth—"How to know God's will," or "Three steps

to conquer stress." Although an important step in applying biblical principles to life is a personal strategy or action plan, application is *not* a simplistic "1 . . . 2 . . . 3 . . ." approach to life.

2. *"Becoming a Christian and then living the Christian life is not a matter of works but of faith."* That statement is true, but application does not mean working one's way to heaven or depending on self instead of God. It does, however, involve personal response to God's Word, everything from "believe on the Lord Jesus Christ," to "go into all the world and preach the gospel." In fact, as James reminds us, "Faith that doesn't show itself by good works is no faith at all—it is dead and useless" (James 2:17).

3. *"God is more interested in our* being *the right kind of people than in our* doing *things for him."* Again, this betrays a misconception of the word *application,* as though it refers to a narrow category of responses. But a personal application might be to draw closer to Christ through worship, prayer, meditation, or study. An application for someone else might involve yielding certain areas of life to Christ's control. Application means obedience, and the Bible is filled with that admonition.

4. *"What people really need is sound theology. This emphasis on action is shallow."* Theologian R. C. Sproul says that Western Christians are "biblically illiterate" and that there is no substitute for solid, biblical theology. I would agree, and certainly actions that are not grounded in the Word of God will be shallow at best. But right thinking should lead to right living. Unfortunately, however, the shift from thinking to acting is not automatic. Many people know a lot about the Bible and may even get *A*'s in theology classes, but they don't allow God's truth to penetrate their hearts. Their head knowledge hasn't filtered down into the rest of their lives.

5. *"Only the Holy Spirit can apply the words of Scripture to a person's life."* Whether written or spoken, Bible applications can never take the place of the Holy Spirit. But there is a place for suggested courses of action, illustrations of how others have put faith into practice, insights into Scripture's timeless truths, and personal

challenges. Consider the evangelist who calls people to give their lives to Christ. He is not taking the place of the Holy Spirit; rather, he is presenting the gospel and then throwing out the challenge to act, to those whom the Holy Spirit is convicting.

AM I READY FOR APPLICATION?

Hopefully by this point you know what application is, are convinced that it is necessary, and understand why making applications can be difficult. Now you're just about ready to dig in to the Word. To be prepared and to overcome any application resistance, ask yourself the following questions.

1. *Am I truly open to the Word of God?* Suppose you were at a party and received word that the most interesting, powerful, and influential person in the world was in the next room and wanted to talk to you. Would you go? Of course you would. The truth is that God himself, the creator and ruler of the universe, wants to meet you in his Word. But you must be willing to enter into open communication with him.

Will you lay aside your concerns, preoccupations, and pursuits to focus on him and his message to you? Will you reset your will so that you can be ready to move? Can you be flexible and responsive? When you take out your Bible, ask yourself, "If I open it and understand it, will I do it? Do I really want to do what God wants?" If you are closed to God, reading his Word will be a waste of time.

Another way to be open is to use a reading program, perhaps even taking you through the entire Bible. Through this the Holy Spirit will spotlight areas that you need to change. Too often Christians concentrate Bible reading in familiar passages. But God may have messages for you in parts of the Bible that you haven't read lately.

2. *Do I have a translation that I understand?* If your Bible translation uses language that you do not use in ordinary conversation, you will have a difficult time seeing how it applies to your everyday life. It would be like trying to understand a Russian Bible after having only a couple of years of Russian in school. You won't be able to understand the meaning of a passage if you're struggling with the language.

In the King James Version, Acts 5:6 reads, "The young men arose, wound him up, and carried him out, and buried him." Even when you understand the context ("him" refers to Ananias, who had just died after lying to Peter and the Holy Spirit), it sounds like "no batteries required" because they "wound him up." By the way, the Authorized King James Version was written in modern English . . . for England in the 1600s.

I won't debate the pros and cons of various versions—many outstanding ones are available. Try using two translations: one a more or less word-for-word (such as the *New American Standard Bible* or the New King James, New Revised Standard, or New International Version), and the other a thought-for-thought translation (such as *The Living Bible,* Today's English Version, or the Contemporary English Version). Tyndale House Publishers has a helpful *NIV/Living Parallel Bible.*

Skim the entire passage in modern, simplified English and then focus on it verse by verse, referring to both translations.

3. *Do I have the right tools?* It is helpful to understand the historical and cultural context of a passage. But even in a modern translation, you will encounter foreign words and concepts. Tools are available to help you dig out the meaning.

A good study Bible (of course I recommend the *Life Application Bible*) and a Bible dictionary should have what you need. As you focus on the verse, the meaning will be more powerful if you see it in context.

4. *Have I expressed my need to God?* Because God knows all your needs and sorrows, you may wonder why you should bother to tell him about them. God does know everything about us, and the Holy Spirit prays for us (Romans 8:26-27). God understands, and yet he wants us to engage our minds as we pray: "I will pray with my spirit, but I will also pray with my mind" (1 Corinthians 14:15, NIV). You will be more ready to apply God's Word to your life if you are sensitive to the areas that desperately need application. And as you pray, God will bring other needs to mind.

If you stop to take a simple spiritual diagnosis before opening the pages of Scripture, you will be more likely to find help. Before you read, ask:

- What conflicts am I facing at home, work, school, or church?
- What resources do I lack (for example, time, energy, money, relationships)?
- What difficult situations am I facing?
- What personal shortcomings am I struggling to overcome?

By expressing your need to God, you will prepare your heart to receive his truth. Verses will seem to jump off the page, and you'll find more applications. Being alert and focusing your attention will help you respond to the directions God gives in the Bible.

If you are open to God's Word, use a translation that you can easily understand, use the right tools, and express your needs to God, you will be ready to apply the Bible. Of course, getting ready is just the first step in reading, understanding, and obeying God's Word. In the next section we will see how to get the Bible off the shelf and into the self!

WORKING IT THROUGH

1. What is the most difficult aspect of Bible application for you?

_____

_____

_____

2. Which of the statements opposing "application" have you heard most often?

_____

_____

_____

How would you respond to someone who thinks that application is unnecessary?

_____

_____

_____

3. What would help you to be more open to God's Word?

_____

_____

_____

4. What Bible study tools do you need to help you understand and apply the Bible to your life? Where and when will you get these tools?

_____

_____

_____

5. What personal needs should you express to God right now?

_____

_____

_____

Chapter at a Glance

People make weak application because:
- Applying the Bible is hard work
- They are afraid
- They don't prepare
- They don't know how

To overcome application resistance:
- Be open to the Word of God
- Use a translation of Scripture that you can easily understand
- Use Bible study tools
- Express your needs to God

PART TWO
Finding
Applications

CHAPTER FOUR

The Pyramid: Up One Side

The church business meeting was unusually tense. After two long discussions, the third agenda item was whether or not to purchase a new chandelier. After the chairman introduced the topic, a man stood to his feet at the back of the room.

"I'm against it!" he declared. "First of all, I can't spell it! Second, no one around here can play one!" He paused briefly.

"And what we really need around here is more light!"

Sometimes when I speak about Bible application I feel like that church chairman, wondering if people really understand the concept. In part one we discussed preparing for applications. We now know what Bible application is, why it's important, how it can be difficult, and how to get ready. That's enough preparation . . . now let's dig in!

Have you ever been gripped by an insight from your Bible study but felt confused about how to live it out?

Have you ever listened to a sermon and silently wondered how the speaker was able to see so many practical applications in a passage that you had just studied?

Have you ever made a personal application that was truly helpful and exciting, and wondered why you didn't have that experience more often?

Have you ever prepared extensively for a small group Bible study and yet found it difficult or nearly impossible to show how the passage was relevant and practical?

Like me, you probably can answer yes to most of those questions. You want to apply the Bible more effectively but aren't sure how. As we have seen, application is the step between *knowing* what the Bible says and *doing* what it says. But while the truths of the Bible never change, life situations do. I have noticed that as my life changes, the old applications don't seem to work anymore. To keep growing in my relationship with Christ, I need to keep applying the Bible to my *new* experiences, thoughts, and feelings.

For example, when I was working for Youth for Christ in the Campus Life ministry, right out of college, I found it relatively easy to apply the passages and teachings in the Bible regarding money. After all, my income was low; and because I was single, my life was simple and my expenses, basic. Then I got married and bought a house. Suddenly my finances were complex, and I found it increasingly difficult and challenging to obey what I would read in the Bible about money matters.

In those first few years of marriage, it was also fairly easy to apply the biblical teachings about the family. Today, however, my two daughters are teenagers, so my need for biblical applications and the difficulty of making them have grown immensely!

Application has become more difficult in both of those areas. I'm less sure of what to do; and when I do know, it's a greater struggle to obey. Moreover, suggested applications that I hear in sermons and read in books don't seem to relate to my life as easily as they used to. My life has become more complex and my problems, more specific and personal. Instead of relying on the applications of others, I need to apply the Bible myself.

While I discovered no simple solution to this problem, I have begun to use a Bible study system that helps immensely. It's called the *Pyramid.* My associates and I originally developed and used a similar system to generate the application notes for the *Life Application Bible.* Using the nine sets of questions in the Pyramid, you will be able to apply the Bible more practically and thoroughly to your personal life situations.

THE PYRAMID

All Bible study methods have the same three basic stages: *Read,
Comprehend,* and *Apply.* At the *Read* stage we answer the question
"What does this say?" At *Comprehend* we answer "What does this
mean?" And at *Apply* we answer "What should I do?" If any of these
stages is missing, we will not fully understand and obey what the
Bible teaches.

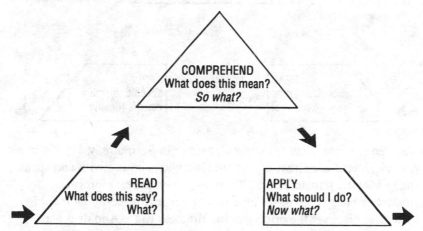

At the *Read* stage, we read a specific passage and try to understand
the story, what is happening. If this stage is underemphasized, we
will not get much out of the study. Our Bible reading will feel dry.

At the *Comprehend* stage, we look for the biblical principles that
transcend time and are transferable. People who neglect this stage
run the risk of misinterpreting, and therefore misapplying, a passage.

At the *Apply* stage, we personalize the truths and think about how
to live them out. Neglecting this stage leads to plastic beliefs, with
insights from Bible study making little or no difference in our lives.

Here's another way to look at the Pyramid.

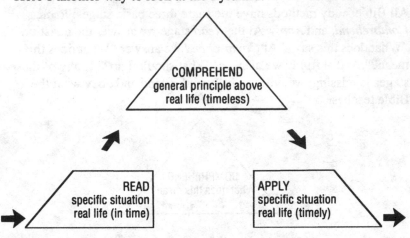

You can see that when we study a passage in Scripture, we begin in a historical, real-life situation, where God was working with and speaking to specific human beings. Then, as we let the text inform us (inductive study), we move up and away from a specific moment in history to discover the principle, the timeless truth. And then we allow that principle to inform us as we move down and back to real life, our daily experience, making timely applications for specific, personal situations.

With a simple, straightforward passage, this may be all the structure we need. But what if we can't see the biblical principles? What if we can't bring them down into our real-life situations?

Of course speaking or writing about the process of studying the Bible is easy; actually doing it takes a lot more work. In fact, sometimes in-depth, application-oriented Bible study can seem impossible. That's because usually we try to climb the Pyramid in just two giant steps. Moving from *Read* to *Comprehend* takes a big jump, as does going from *Comprehend* to *Apply*. It's no wonder that many Christians get tired and stop trying.

When a task seems too big or unmanageable, it is helpful to break the task down into smaller steps. When each step is manageable, we can make better progress and feel a sense of real accomplishment.

Check out the Pyramid below, which includes additional, more manageable steps.

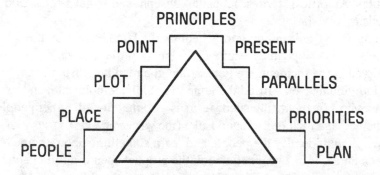

Using these smaller steps, we will be able to climb the Bible study Pyramid much more easily. Let's take them one at a time.

1. PEOPLE

One reason that *People* is the first step is because it is usually quite easy to identify the people in the passage simply by reading the text, especially in historical narratives such as Genesis or Matthew. An old Chinese proverb says, "Every journey begins with the first step." Once we take that step, we're on our way.

People is also an important step because we, the readers, are people too. And as we read, we discover that because human nature hasn't changed over the centuries, neither have human struggles and problems.

The people include all the characters in the passage, those actively taking part and those mentioned. Sometimes no specific individuals or groups will be named in a chapter or section of a book, such as in Proverbs or Romans. But we shouldn't forget the author and the original audience. They are people too—although we may not read about these individuals, we know they are there, watching and listening in. Also, God should be included in the *People* category. Here are two examples of *People* in the Bible.

Exodus 13 records Moses' speech to the children of Israel as they began to leave Egypt and head for the Promised Land. The key characters are Moses (giving the speech and writing the book), the nation of Israel, and Pharaoh. Also mentioned in the chapter are Canaanites, Hittites, Amorites, Hivites, Jebusites, Joseph, and Israel's sons. God also is involved.

Acts 3:1-11 tells about Peter's healing the lame beggar by the temple gate. The people mentioned in the narrative, actively involved in the incident, are Peter, John, the man lame from birth, the individuals who carried the lame man to the temple gate, and those who saw the man healed. Jesus is also mentioned. Other people in the passage include God and Luke (the writer of Acts).

We should identify the people and learn something about them. For example, if in a prophetic book the prophet spends a full chapter condemning a nation we've never heard of, we should use a Bible dictionary or a study Bible to find out more about what those people were like.

In addition to identifying the people in the passage, it is important to identify *with* the people. This will help us with both interpretation and application. In fact, at every step in our climb up the Pyramid we should ask "identification" questions. Here are questions to ask when identifying the people in a passage and identifying with them:

● Who are all of the people in this passage?
● How are these people like people in my world?
● What characteristics in myself do I see represented in these people?

2. PLACE

This step helps put the passage in its original setting, the historical and cultural context. By taking this step, we will be able to see, hear, and feel what we read in the text.

We can learn about *Place* in a study Bible or commentary, or by looking up the book in a Bible dictionary. Knowing about the city of Corinth will illuminate a passage in 1 Corinthians. Learning about Israel, Judah, and the political, economic, and religious status of Hosea's audience will help us understand his book. The more we know about the culture, history, and problems of the people in the passage, the more we will be able to find parallels to our lives today.

It is also helpful to skim the entire book of the Bible, familiarizing ourselves with the outline and key themes. The book of Job is an example of how important this is. If we did not realize that the miserable comforters Bildad, Eliphaz, and Zophar were bringing not God's words but their own, we might agree that Job's suffering was caused by his own sin. (Note: skimming the entire book will also help us with *Plot,* the next step on our climb.)

Of course, we also should read the immediate context of any passage (the surrounding verses). Often this will help us understand the meaning of unknown words and difficult concepts. Usually what the author said previously or subsequently will shed light on the passage being studied.

Here, as with *People,* it is important to compare the setting of this passage with our own place in time and in the world. We may discover that the Israelites who crossed the Red Sea were "baby boomers," the products of a surge in population . . . or that Ephesus had many similarities with a major city near where we live.

For the *Place* step, we can ask:

● What is the setting of this passage?
● What are the significant details in the history, culture, and geography?
● What are the similarities to my world?

3. PLOT

The third step of our climb up the Bible study Pyramid is to consider the plot of the passage. *Plot* answers "What's happening?" In other words, we should be looking for what is going on among people or between God and people. Usually we can discover this by the context of the passage and book. A study Bible or commentary will also help us understand the plot.

The plot is easy to unravel in a Gospel or any historical book. But a story line may not be apparent in some books of the Bible, as in 2 John or Philemon. But understanding the conflict that underlies a passage will help unlock additional applications. Every book of the Bible either contains a conflict or speaks directly to one.

The questions to ask for *Plot* are:

● What is happening in this passage?
● What is the conflict or tension?
● What would I have done in this situation?
● How is this similar to what is happening in my life or in the world today?

Recently I used *People, Place,* and *Plot* to gain penetrating insights from Numbers 17, the story of Aaron's staff budding. The Lord wanted to stop the constant grumbling of the people against Moses and Aaron. After the twelve leaders of Israel gave their staffs to Moses, he placed them before the Lord. Aaron's staff not only budded, but it also blossomed and produced almonds. Through this dramatic incident, everyone could plainly see that Aaron had been appointed by God.

I understood what the passage said. Then I took a few minutes to formulate some of the connections between this event from ancient times and my own life.

In terms of *People,* I saw that these were not just ordinary men, but the leaders of the twelve tribes of Israel. I certainly am not a leader on this level myself, but I can identify some of the leaders in the Christian world today. I would be upset if they were grumbling against God as these men in Numbers had done. Then I realized that I also grumble against some of God's appointed leaders in the world. In the story, I wouldn't have been one of the leaders, but I might have supported one and grumbled right along with him.

At the *Place* step, besides reviewing what I knew about the exodus and the wilderness, I saw that this event occurred shortly after two rebellions for which the people had been severely punished. These were no minor grievances in Exodus 17—the bitterness against Moses and Aaron was deeply rooted.

With *Plot,* I noticed that one of the twelve leaders, Aaron, was being selected from among the group for special service. It is easy for tension to develop when a peer is promoted. I then realized that I, too, was feeling somewhat resentful of a friend who had recently received a nice promotion and pay raise (and I thought he was less qualified than I). Did the other tribal leaders think that Aaron was less qualified for the special responsibilities than they were? Suddenly I was involved in the passage and was ready to interpret the meaning.

In essence, during these first three steps, we go back in time to understand the passage and to see ourselves in it. Now, as we approach the top of the Pyramid, we stand above time, looking for the timeless truths. This is not a subjective process—the Bible expresses objective truth. So we must determine what a passage means, not what we wish it to mean. Perhaps you have heard a person in a Bible study say something like, "Well, to me this verse means. . . ." Some individuals talk as if interpretation is a very subjective exercise. Interestingly, those people probably would not approach an instruction manual for computer software in the same manner. Instead, they would work diligently to determine the objective meaning of the words on the page. They would never consider making up a meaning that suits them. They would dig deeper to understand the correct meaning of the manual. While we should read the Bible with feeling, we should interpret it as a book that contains objective truth.

The three steps that get us over the top in interpretation are *Point* (understanding the original message), *Principles* (determining the timeless truths), and *Present* (describing contemporary significance).

4. POINT

Before we can determine what something in the Bible means for us today, we must first ascertain the meaning for the original audience. The events recorded in the Bible happened to real people at specific times in history. Real audiences heard the parables, and real churches received the epistles. Therefore, we should carefully consider the cultural context (what we learned at the *People, Place,* and *Plot* steps) to find the particular lessons that God wanted to teach those people. In effect, the *Point* was the application for the original audience.

To determine the *Point,* we can ask:

● What was the intended message for the original audience?
● What did the people in the passage learn?

- What did God want them to do?
- What was God's solution to the problem?

Perhaps you have read about a religious zealot somewhere who actually tried to cut off a hand or gouge out an eye as an application of Matthew 5:29-30. Did Jesus really mean that we should mutilate ourselves as a means of holy living? Did Jesus expect his original listeners to apply his message that way and suddenly chop off their hands or poke out their eyes? No! Jesus used an extreme example (hyperbole, or overstatement) to teach that avoiding sin may demand painful sacrifices.

Or perhaps you have been confused when reading passages in the epistles about eating meat. For example, in 1 Corinthians 8:13, Paul wrote, "Therefore, if what I eat causes my brother to fall into sin, I will never eat meat again, so that I will not cause him to fall" (NIV). Was Paul saying that Christians should be vegetarians? No (see 8:8-9). Although meat was certainly involved in the controversy, Paul was making a point about being sensitive to the tender consciences of new believers in Christ. The meat in question had previously been offered to idols.

A clear understanding of the *Point* can prevent damaging misapplications and is invaluable for determining the timeless truths in the passage.

5. PRINCIPLES

After finding the *Point,* the meaning for the original audience, our next step is to determine what transferable principles are embedded in the passage. This step is stated in plural form because often more than one principle can be found.

The distinction between *Point* and *Principle* can be easy to miss because they are closely related. The principles usually connect with the original point of the passage and may even be identical to the point for the original audience. For example, in the teaching about cutting off a hand (Matthew 5:29-30), the principle is the same as the point: avoiding sin may involve painful sacrifices. The point of 1

John 3:11-24 to the original audience and the principle for us are the same: love one another.

At times, of course, the principle and point differ. Let's look again at 1 Corinthians 8:13 where Paul wrote about eating meat that had been offered to idols. As I mentioned earlier, Paul was teaching the Corinthian believers to be sensitive to the feelings and tender faith of new followers of Christ. These men and women had come out of paganism and were deeply offended by anything that reminded them of their former days and way of life. Paul's point was that eating meat that had previously been offered to idols or "blessed" by pagan priests was wrong, even though there was nothing wrong with the meat itself (in fact, usually that was the best meat available). It was wrong because eating this meat would harm the tender faith of a Christian brother or sister.

Today, the meat in our supermarkets usually is not divided into "idol blessed" and "regular," so meat is not the issue for us. But there are other activities and actions that could be covered by this biblical principle. Young believers can be hurt in other ways. The principle is universal and timeless: mature Christians must be very careful about offending younger, immature believers. Even though we may be free to do something, at times it is better to refrain. The point (application) differs greatly, from era to era and culture to culture.

There are also times when a biblical principle will relate *indirectly* to the passage. For example, we can glean principles about evangelism by observing how Jesus and the disciples spread the gospel, even though "how to evangelize" is not being taught directly in the passage. Consider the lessons learned from the lives of Jeremiah, Hosea, Ezekiel, and other prophets who obeyed God despite tremendous inconvenience, persecution, suffering, and cost. And think of what we can learn about God's character by seeing his reactions to idolatry, greed, injustice, and other sins and his unfailing love for his people.

To surface the *Principles,* we can ask:

- What is the message for all of humankind?
- What are the timeless truths?
- What is the moral of the story?

In each Bible passage, you may find more than one transferable principle. These principles are the distilled essence of a passage. Like standing at the top of a great Egyptian pyramid, we can see for miles around, and the insights are exhilarating. It would be tempting to end our journey at the top—to stay there and just take in the sights. But to apply the Bible, we must go down the other side, back into real life.

While each passage will have one primary meaning, each passage will have a wide range of applications. The path to the top of the Pyramid narrows to a single point and a few principles, but the paths on the way down are diverse and varied.

In the next chapter, we travel down, back to where we live.

WORKING IT THROUGH
Turn to Acts 27:27-44 and climb the Bible study Pyramid, writing the information at each step. Limit each answer here to one or two sentences or phrases.

PEOPLE

_____

_____

_____

PLACE

_____

_____

_____

PLOT

_____

_____

_____

POINT

_____

_____

_____

PRINCIPLES

_____

_____

_____

Here are some possible answers for Acts 27:27-44 on the Bible study Pyramid.

PEOPLE: Luke (the author, included in "we" in the passage), Paul, the sailors, other prisoners, soldiers guarding the other prisoners, the centurion guarding Paul (Julius, see 27:1), God

PLACE: on ship, sailing across the Adriatic Sea (27:27), near the island of Malta (28:1), during a terrible storm, as Paul and other Roman prisoners were being taken to Rome for trial; the journey was undertaken "after the Fast" (27:9, NIV), so it was in October, a time when dangerous storms could arise suddenly

PLOT: Paul had warned that the trip would be disastrous (27:9-10), but the pilot and centurion didn't listen and determined to sail anyway. When the terrible storm arose, Paul encouraged everyone (27:22) and told them what to do; this time the Roman crew listened (27:31-38). Paul also thanked God in front of everyone (27:35). When the ship began to break up, the soldiers were about to kill their prisoners (so they wouldn't escape), but the centurion guarding Paul stopped them from carrying out their plan (27:43).

POINT: Paul was confident of God's protection and care, even during a life-threatening storm. This confidence freed Paul to encourage others, even his captors, and to give a clear testimony of his faith in Christ.

PRINCIPLES: God is present and in control in all of our storms; we can take courage and hope because we know that God is with us and he cares for us. Even when we are going through difficult times, we should encourage and help others and give clear evidence of our faith.

Chapter at a Glance

People
- Who are all of the people in this passage?
- How are these people like people in my world?
- What characteristics in myself do I see represented in these people?

Place
- What is the setting of this passage?
- What are significant details in the history, culture, and geography?
- What are similarities to my world?

Plot
- What is happening in this passage?
- What is the conflict or tension?
- What would I have done in this situation?

- How is this similar to what is happening in my life or in the world today?

Point
- What was the intended message for the original audience?
- What did the people in the passage learn?
- What did God want them to do?
- What was God's solution to the problem?

Principles
- What is the message for all of humankind?
- What are the timeless truths?
- What is the moral of the story?

CHAPTER FIVE
The Pyramid: Down the Other Side

With cautious baby steps I inched toward the chair lift. *I can do it,* I almost whispered out loud as I tried to psych myself up. The ski lessons had gone well. I was proud of my beginner's prowess on the slippery, sloping bunny hill. But it was time to move on and upward, and I was determined to try. Soon I was in line . . . then I was next . . . then suddenly I was airborne, whisked up the side of the mountain. Buoyed with renewed confidence (having conquered the dreaded chair lift), I relaxed and enjoyed the view. In a few minutes, the top came into view—the end of the beginning of my new adventure. As I carefully left the lift, wobbling a bit but without falling, a new terror struck—I had to descend, go down, actually *ski!* I stalled as long as possible: adjusting my goggles, taking in the majestic, panoramic view, casually conversing with fellow "skiers" while leaning on my poles and looking cool. But I knew that couldn't last. Eventually the moment of truth would come when I would have to push off and down. And it did . . . and I became a skier.

I won't share the details of my first descent (they probably have been long suppressed), but eventually I made it down the mountain. But what if I had stayed at the base and had never made the climb? Or what if I had ended my trip at the top and had hitched a ride home on the ski patrol's snowmobile? Certainly I would have had an experience in the Rockies, perhaps even an enjoyable experience . . . but I wouldn't have skied.

In the same way, Bible study must be more than reading, and even more than interpretation. Climbing up the Pyramid is only half the process. We must come down. We must come back to earth, to application and real life.

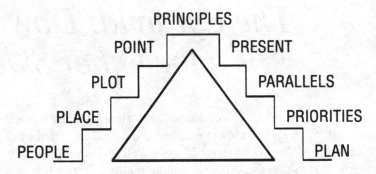

PRINCIPLES

POINT — PRESENT

PLOT — PARALLELS

PLACE — PRIORITIES

PEOPLE — PLAN

In the last chapter, we climbed the steps entitled *People, Place, Plot, Point,* and *Principles.* Now we begin our descent.

6. PRESENT

The first step on the downward side is *Present.* This step expands the areas of application for the *Point* and *Principles* that we have extracted from the passage under study. In fact, a different kind of thinking is required, because we are expanding possibilities and adding our lives to the principles. Here we describe the significant implications of these timeless truths for life at home, school, place of work, church, and neighborhood.

To bring a biblical principle into the *Present,* we can ask:

- What does this principle mean for my society and culture?
- How is this relevant?
- What back then is similar to today?
- How can I make the timeless truth timely?

The *Present* step brings the truth into our context, into today's world, into the here and now. This is where we try to determine what in our society and culture might be similar to washing feet or eating meat offered to idols. It is also helpful to think of possible implications for various types of people (for example, parents, children, teachers, supervisors, employees, business owners, church leaders, etc.).

In James 1:19 the point and principle are simple and straightforward: Christians should "listen much, speak little, and not become angry." To bring this truth into the present, take a moment to think about the possible implications for home, school, work, church, neighborhood, and world.

- *Home:* Parents should take time to listen to their children (and children to their parents) and avoid becoming angry and abusing their kids.
- *School:* Teachers should listen to their students; students should listen to teachers; classmates should listen to each other.
- *Work:* Supervisors should not fly into a rage with their employees, but instead they should listen to them; workers should listen to supervisors and to each other.
- *Church:* Members should not react emotionally to issues, and some should not dominate the fellowship time after the worship service; leaders should listen to the congregation.
- *Neighborhood:* We should not bicker with neighbors; instead we should listen when told of a problem or concern; we should stay clear of neighborhood gossip.
- *World:* We should not become easily angered by poor service in a store, restaurant, or other place of business; we should not react angrily when cut off in traffic.

While the meaning for the original audience and the principles may be clear and evident in a verse such as this, the implications for the present are rich and varied. This step is helpful because you will find more areas where a principle will apply to your own life if you first take a few minutes to consider the implications in *all* areas of life. This is *general* application.

Personal application is the next phase of the process. A Bible truth or insight will not make a difference in our lives unless we take it personally. These final steps will help us do that. As we descend the Pyramid, we carry the principles back to where we live. This phase helps us determine what kind of person we must become and what we must do as a result of the truth we have encountered in the Bible. Gaining the insight is not enough; we must also think, pray, and plan to put it into practice.

7. PARALLELS

The personalizing process begins with *Parallels*—identifying personal application areas. I find that I unintentionally divide my life into compartments, such as home, work, church, and so forth. Thus lessons I learn at work may not be applied at home, and I may behave differently at church than I do at work. The *Parallels* step helps us examine all areas of our lives to see how the truth applies in every one.

This step is similar to *Present,* except that it is very personal, addressing specific life situations, fears, hopes, and relationships. This is the time to explore *all* the areas of life where the truth might apply. In this step, we may discover one or many specific applications.

To find the *Parallels,* we can ask:

● What does this truth mean for me?
● Where are my areas of need, conviction, and opportunity?
● Where in my life might this truth possibly apply?

Sometimes the parallels are not evident at first. Proverbs 12:15, for example, says that a wise man listens to advice and a fool does not. At first, I thought that there was not much in this proverb for me to apply since I rarely refuse to listen to advice.

I started looking for personal parallels for this verse by first noting that everyone acts foolishly once in a while, including me. Next I thought about recent times when I had ignored good advice. As I considered the areas of my life, my thoughts turned to home, work, and church. I began to remember times when I failed to heed the counsel of others, especially my wife.

I thought of the time when Gail advised me not to make a pronouncement or speech to our daughter during a mini-crisis at school, but instead to be quiet and listen to her side of the story. Because I have worked for many years with teenagers, I thought I knew how to handle the one in our house. So ignoring my wife's wise counsel, I jumped into the fray with both feet and immediately escalated the conflict.

Remembering that incident helped me understand that I don't consider advice as carefully as I thought I did, especially in family matters. I began to realize that this proverb *did apply* to me and could help me be wiser at home.

After surfacing application areas, we may find one or more hot spots that need attention. These may be areas of outright disobedience, dangerous temptations, potential problems, or attitudes or behavior needing correction. After surfacing parallel areas, we should select one that we consider to be the most important and move down to the next step on the Pyramid.

8. PRIORITIES

This step involves looking at how we should change on the inside in order to change on the outside. It means stopping to think about the work God wants to do *in* our lives before determining specific behaviors to change. At times this will involve considerable reflection.

To help examine the implications of a biblical truth for our *Priorities,* we can ask:

- How should I adjust my priorities?
- What should I change about my values, beliefs, attitudes, or character?
- What about my thoughts and motives should change?
- What kind of person does God want me to become?

When studying the foot-washing passage (John 13:12-15) for example, I thought of my church and how we serve each other. We

meet in a school, so every Sunday we have to set up the auditorium
for worship and the classrooms for Sunday school. This task is
rotated monthly among groups of families, called Growth Groups.
Church setup is a very important, and often difficult, service that gets
very little recognition. I began to feel guilty because at the time I
wasn't involved in a Growth Group, so I was never asked to help
with this necessary task. I decided that God wanted me to learn how
to serve others by volunteering to help with setup even though I
didn't have to.

In the process, God also began to point out how I tend to avoid
demeaning, dirty, and thankless tasks. Instead, I enjoy serving in the
limelight. I saw that God wanted me to be more other-centered
instead of self-centered.

This is one of the more difficult steps with certain applications.
The heart can be deceptive. We can become experts at rationalizing
and excusing the way we are. Fortunately, the Holy Spirit works in
us, pointing out what is displeasing to God in our lives. When we
find something in ourselves that is lacking or that needs change,
we are personalizing the biblical principle at the highest level.
Then, after pinpointing problem areas, we must *act* to see our lives
change.

9. PLAN

This is the last step in the Bible study process: actually doing what
God has told us to do. We put truth into practice by determining to
change and then making plans to live differently. The planning skills
that we use in other areas of life will prove useful here. (Note: we
will look at this more closely in chapter 10.) Planning involves
selecting a goal, breaking it down into bite-size pieces, and getting
going.

To help us *Plan*, we can ask:

- What does God want me to *do* about what I have learned?
- What steps will get me to that goal?
- What should be my first step? How can I get started?

There are two types of plans: *intentional* and *conditional.* Intentional plans are step-by-step guides for taking action. These are similar to strategies, plans, or lists that people use to accomplish specific tasks and goals. For example, if someone was serious about trying to lose weight, he or she would probably design a weight-reduction plan that would involve exercise and diet. The plan for someone who wanted to obtain a real estate license would involve talking with a real estate broker, signing up for classes, and so forth.

Intentional plans contain action steps within the individual's control. An intentional plan might have the statement "I will" followed by a To Do list in chronological order (a "1 . . . 2 . . . 3 . . ." format).

An intentional plan for me for applying John 13:12-15 might be:

I want to serve the church by helping set-up for services this month. To do this, I will:

1. Call the church office to find out which Growth Group is assigned for this month.
2. Call the Growth Group leader and tell him/her of my intentions.
3. Show up next Sunday morning at 8:00 to help set up.

Conditional plans are anticipated responses to situations that might arise. Usually they follow an "If . . . , then . . ." format. We use conditional plans continually in our daily lives: "If I see Chad, then I'll tell him hello for you"; "If I can't find a parking place near the store, then I'll use the parking garage two blocks away"; "If this meeting ends early, then I'll make that sales call on the way home"; "If the store has a sale, then I will buy that sweater." Jesus said, "If someone hits you, then turn the other cheek."

In applying the Bible, conditional plans are needed for avoiding specific temptations and responding to specific opportunities. A teenager might say, "If I am offered a drink, then I will say 'No.'" A businessman might write, "If Ed asks me about the Bible on my desk or about anything spiritual, then I'll share my faith with him." A conditional plan for me for the passage on listening to advice (Proverbs 12:15) might be: "If Gail makes a suggestion about how to act toward our girls, then I will listen."

Sometimes the application for a passage will lead to both types of plans. For example, my plans for applying the principle of love in 1 Corinthians 13:4-7 might be:

I will be more loving toward Gail by:
1. Not complaining when I come home from work
2. Clearing the table after dinner
3. Bringing her roses next week

And if she has had a bad day, then I will listen to her feelings and not argue with her.

When neither the "If . . . , then . . ." nor the "1 . . . 2 . . . 3 . . ." formats seems to work for one of our applications, we probably do not yet have our concrete actions clearly worked out and should go back to *Present, Parallels,* or *Priorities.* Every practical application will be one of these two types.

The Bible study Pyramid is a step-by-step system for generating personal applications from the Bible. As we climb up one side, on the *Read* steps, we dig into the Bible to see what it says and means. At the top, *Comprehend,* we look for the objective truth so that we identify the timeless biblical principles and avoid reading something into the text that is not there. Then, as we move back down the other side, on the *Apply* steps, we personalize our insights and put them into practice. Although this system can be used anywhere in the Bible, certain steps work better in certain types of passages than others. We will take a close look at the various types of biblical literature in chapters 8 and 9.

The Pyramid may seem complex at first because there are so many steps, but it will become easier as you use it. You will quickly see how your natural application abilities fit into each of the steps. You will be able to pinpoint the steps where you are naturally strong and those that need additional work. As your skills improve with practice, you will be able to apply the Bible more completely, thoroughly, and effectively.

WORKING IT THROUGH
Continue the study of Acts 27:27-44 that you began last chapter and climb down the steps of the Pyramid.

PRESENT

_____

_____

_____

PARALLELS

_____

_____

PRIORITIES

_____

_____

_____

PLAN

_____

_____

_____

Here's the way I might have answered at each step:

PRESENT: I'm not a prisoner of a foreign government, being taken to trial by boat in a terrible storm, but I do have rough seas in my life. I have a problem with one of my company's clients, a conflict with my daughter's basketball coach, and other difficult situations.

PARALLELS: The main parallel to my life is Paul's attitude in the middle of the crisis—he remained calm, gave instructions, encouraged everyone, and was a positive example of a follower of Christ. In both the problem at work and the one at school, I need to explain my case calmly and confidently. But in doing this, I should be positive and helpful, not negative, hateful, or divisive.

PRIORITIES: My natural tendency is to get angry and tell someone off when I think he or she is wrong, or to shout orders without being sensitive to the feelings of others. I think that God wants me to be more patient and understanding. Perhaps through the *way* I communicate, I can be a positive witness for Christ.

PLAN: With the conflict at school, I need to speak with the athletic director and/or the coach directly (not write a letter) and explain my position carefully, calmly, and with concern for the feelings of the coach. I will:
1. Call the athletic director and set up an appointment to see him.
2. Write out my points beforehand so I won't get off on a tangent and get upset.
3. Meet with the athletic director and carefully explain my position, letting him know that I still respect him and the coach as people.
   In the problem with a client, I need to be ready to respond when the situation arises. *If* I see the CEO or CFO, *then* I need to encourage them and keep our discussions on a positive plane rather than point out problems and friction in our working relationship.

Chapter at a Glance

Present
- What does this principle mean for my society and culture?
- How is this relevant?
- What back then is similar to today?
- How can I make the timeless truth timely?

Parallels
- What does this truth mean for me?
- Where are my areas of need, conviction, and opportunity?
- Where in my life might this truth possibly apply?

Priorities
- How should I adjust my priorities?
- What should I change about my values, beliefs, attitudes, or character?
- What about my thoughts and motives should change?
- What kind of person does God want me to become?

Plan
- What does God want me to *do* about what I have learned?
- What steps will get me to that goal?
- What should be my first step? How can I get started?

Areas for application:
- Home ● School ● Work ● Church
- Neighborhood ● World

Types of application plans:
- Intentional: "I will reach my goal by taking the following steps."
- Conditional: "If . . . , then I will . . ."

CHAPTER SIX

The Window: Looking In

ODE TO A WINDOW

Oh thou clear guardian of light
Its rays you permit to pass,
A silent sentinel at night
Guarding with your eye of glass.
Even when the winds do race
You shelter us from storm,
And provide a watching place
To view the shadowy form.

This may not be great poetry, but the ode does highlight the value of windows in modern life. Because of windows, we can look in, and we can look out. Remember pressing your face against the window-pane during a spring rainstorm? You could almost feel the water running down the outside surface, yet you were dry. You could see trees swaying from the winds and flowers bending from the downpour.

Or how about those weekend trips with your family to Grandma and Grandpa's house? As you pulled into the driveway, you could see their smiling faces through the window, awaiting your arrival.

This chapter and the next will explain another helpful window. It is a window into Scripture and into our lives—the Application Window. This study method is presented as another approach for studying the Scriptures and finding applications. Many people find the Bible study Pyramid extremely helpful for individual study and for teaching the Bible. The Application Window has proven to be quite helpful to ministers in their sermon preparation.

APPLICATION WINDOW

	People's Need/Problem	God's Action/Solution	People's Response/Obedience
THEN	1.	2.	3.
NOW	4.	5.	6.
ME	7.	8.	9.

The Application Window is divided into nine windowpanes. In this chapter, we will fill in the first two rows as we look through this Window into Scripture. In the next chapter, we will fill in the third row as we look out from Scripture, through the Window and into our lives. Whether our text is a verse, a paragraph, or a chapter, the Application Window can help us move from reading Bible words and learning their meanings to discovering God's Word and his message for us, today.

In this chapter and the next, we will look at two short passages of Scripture to illustrate how the Application Window works. These are Judges 2:10-15 and 1 Peter 1:3-9. I suggest you open your Bible and read these two passages, and then refer to them as we fill in the Window.

Focusing on our text, let's fill in each pane in the Window, starting with the row marked *Then*. The purpose of this row is to put the passage in its historical and cultural context. *Then* refers to the time when the incident or story occurred, or when the passage was written. Commentaries and other resource materials will be very helpful here.

	People's Need/Problem	God's Action/Solution	People's Response/Obedience
THEN	1.	2.	3.

Our objective for the first pane (#1) is to determine *People's Need or Problem* back *Then*. Questions to ask for this pane are:

● Who needed help?
● What was going on?
● What was the problem?

In Judges 2:10-15, a passage about Israel and idol worship, it would be good to know what the people were like and what God had already told them about worshiping idols. It would also help to know about the idols—which ones were involved, how they were worshiped, and why they caused the Jews such problems.

The problem may not be quite so clear or easy to discern. That's where a study Bible or a commentary will be a valuable resource. In 1 Peter 1:3-9, for example, the people needing help were the Jewish believers in Christ who had been scattered throughout the Roman Empire and who were being persecuted unmercifully by Emperor Nero. In fact, Peter was probably executed shortly after writing the second of his two letters (2 Peter). Peter did not include all those details in his letter, but they are an important part of the context.

Whether or not the past problem or conflict is obvious, we need to take time to find it. We must know the problem to understand the solution.

This leads to pane #2. Here the objective is to determine *God's Action or Solution* to the people's need or problem back *Then*. It is vital that we see God's action and find his solution—whatever God does is always right and good. Important questions to ask include:

- How did God react?
- What did God do?
- What did God want the people to do?

Looking again at Judges 2:10-15, our answers would describe God's anger and include a description of God's punishment. God reacted to his people's refusal to obey him by removing his protection from Israel, thus allowing enemies to defeat and plunder the nation. God's desire was that his people worship him alone and not the worthless gods of the nations around them.

Please note that a Bible passage may not describe an immediate and specific reaction from God through immediate blessings or sudden catastrophes. At times we find God promising a *future* reaction or solution. Also, in most of the incidents recorded in the Bible, God did not appear visibly or speak audibly. Instead, God spoke through chosen human beings such as prophets and apostles or simply through previous messages in his Word. So we may have to look a little deeper to see God's reaction.

In 1 Peter 1:3-9, God was telling the persecuted Christians, through Peter, that he was allowing them to experience trials and grief in order to test their trust and commitment. Regardless of the circumstances, they were to remain strong in their faith, confident, secure, and joyful, knowing that their salvation was sure.

After describing the people's problem and God's action, we come to pane #3, *People's Response or Obedience* back *Then*. Our objective for this pane is to determine how the people who received God's message responded to their problem and to God's solution. To help find this answer, we can ask:

● How did the people receive God's message?
● How did the people respond to God's solution? What did they do to obey or disobey him?
● How did God want the people to respond?

In Judges 2, God wanted the people of Israel to forsake their idols and turn back and worship him alone. This passage begins a description of an often-repeated cycle in Jewish history:

1. God would bless his people with peace and prosperity.
2. The people would become complacent and then turn away from God to idols and other sins.
3. God would warn his people about their sin and eventually punish them.
4. The people would repent and ask God for help.
5. God would deliver his people from their enemies and bring them prosperity and peace once again.
6. Then they would become complacent and sin again.

On and on the cycle would go. Here we find that because the people *did not* turn away from their idols, God punished them (as we saw under #2). This punishment led to "great distress" (Judges 2:15, NIV). In the next verse we read how God responded to his people's distress by raising up judges to deliver them from their enemies.

Regarding the passage in 1 Peter, we don't know from Scripture how the recipients of Peter's letter received God's message—the text does not tell us their reactions. From church history, however, we do know that at this time thousands of Christians went to martyrs' deaths, praising God and steadfastly refusing to renounce their faith in Christ. Undoubtedly many of them had been encouraged by Peter's letters and his faithful example.

This row is entitled *Then* because the focus is on the past—the historical, cultural, and social context of the text under study. When we fill in these three panes in the Application Window, we have completed the *Read* and *Understand* stages discussed in chapter 1. The next stage is to fill in the second row, moving from the past to the present, seeing the relevance of the passage and discovering the biblical principles involved. This is the *Comprehend* stage from chapter 1.

	People's Need/Problem	God's Action/Solution	People's Response/Obedience
THEN	1.	2.	3.
NOW	4.	5.	6.

It is important to remember, however, that as we answer questions for a pane in the *Now* row, our answers must be consistent with what we learned in the *Then* row, above. In other words, the lessons and biblical principles must come *out of* the text—we must be careful not to read our ideas into it. Nowhere is this more important than in this first *Now* pane. Here we should not merely describe our current needs and problems. Instead, we should try *to see ourselves in the story* and see how the people back *Then* were like us today. Every passage of Scripture has possible applications for us, but not every passage has an application for every one of our problems and needs. We must let God speak to us through his Word.

As we look through windowpane #4, therefore, our objective is to determine how *People's Needs and Problems* of today are similar to what the people in the text faced back then. We know there are tremendous differences, but in what ways are our struggles, dreams, pressures, and society similar to those of the people back then? To help find this answer, we can ask:

● With whom in the passage do I identify?
● What tension, problem, conflict, or need sounds familiar?
● How are the people in the story like us, like me?

In answering those questions for Judges 2:10-15, we might describe how easy it is for us to take God's love and blessings for granted, to become complacent in our relationship with him. And although most people in our society don't worship statues made of wood, stone, or metal, other "idols" compete for God's place in our lives—money, relationships, and careers, to name just a few.

Considering 1 Peter 1:3-9, we can readily identify current, personal trials. Although not nearly as severe as those suffered by first-century Christians, the persecutions that we suffer for our faith are just as real and can cause us to struggle or to doubt. There is continual tension between making a public stand for Christ and staying silent to ensure personal comfort and status within a peer group. Here it could be helpful to imagine how we might react during a very tough test of faith. How would we come through the refining process?

At this point the Bible passage begins to come to life.

The second windowpane in the *Now* row (#5) is for seeing *God's Action or Solution* to our need or problem today. This is where we begin to discover the timeless truth. We should be looking for the biblical principle that applied back then, applies here and now, and applies in the future. To correctly fill in this pane, we can ask:

● What is God's answer to this question today?
● What is God's solution to our problem?
● What is God doing now?

When it comes to idols (Judges 2), the principle is clear: God wants people, especially his people, to love and serve only him, and he will use drastic means to bring us back to him.

Regarding persecution (1 Peter 1), God continues to hold out hope for all who follow him: our inheritance is sure; we will come through these trials; we will be saved; our faith and future hope should be a source of deep joy.

Notice how much easier it becomes to answer these questions as we progress through the Window. In fact, right now I'm sure you could fill in pane #6 very quickly. In this last pane of the *Now* row, the focus is on action and obedience, looking for how God wants people to respond to his *Solution/Action* described in #5. This pane focuses on answering the question "So what?" To do this, we can ask:

- How does God want people to receive his message?
- How does God want us to react?
- What should people do?

For our discussion of idols, the point is that God wants his people to resist all religious and cultural idols and to love and worship him alone, rejecting anything that might take his place.

In the study of 1 Peter, the principle is that God wants his people to persevere through their trials and persecutions. We are to stay strong in the faith, we are to focus on the reality of God's love and our future hope, and we are to see our present struggles as part of God's refining process.

Having completed the *Then* and *Now* rows of the Window, we are right on the verge of application. This brings us to filling in the last row, which we'll do in the next chapter.

WORKING IT THROUGH

Turn to Hebrews and look at chapter 7 through the Application Window, writing the information in each pane of the *Then* and *Now* rows. You can take the whole chapter, a paragraph, or a short passage.

	People's Need/Problem	God's Action/Solution	People's Response/Obedience
THEN			
NOW			

Here are some possible answers:

	People's Need/Problem	God's Action/Solution	People's Response/Obedience
THEN	Hebrew Christians in danger of falling back into Judaism—falling away from their faith. Why? Hard for them to accept that Christ is completely sufficient for salvation.	God used author of H. to demonstrate the superiority of Christ, how he alone is sufficient for salvation. Goes on to show Christ's credentials to be our high priest, using Melchizedek as an example.	• Persevere • Grow • mature in their faith, study, & understand just why Christ is sufficient for salvation.
NOW	Most of us don't have an *old* religion to fall back into, but there are several *new* religions that entice us: the New Age movement surrounds us, permeating all areas of our society—TV, schools, business, magazines, books, etc.	Through his Word, authors, & preachers, God is demonstrating the superiority of Jesus Christ over all religions. We must communicate this clearly & convincingly.	• Persevere. • Don't get side-tracked; don't get away from reading the bible and searching out its truths. • Don't water down its message by accommodating faith to New Age thinking.

Chapter at a Glance

People's Need/Problem—Then
- Who needed help?
- What was going on?
- What was the problem?

God's Action/Solution—Then
- How did God react?
- What did God do?
- What did God want the people to do?

People's Response/Obedience—Then
- How did the people receive God's message?
- How did the people respond to (obey or disobey) God's solution?
- How did God want the people to respond?

People's Need/Problem—Now
- With whom in the passage do I identify?
- What tension, problem, conflict, or need sounds familiar?
- How are the people in the story like us, like me?

God's Action/Solution—Now
- What is God's answer to this question today?
- What is God's solution to our problem?
- What is God doing now?

People's Response/Obedience—Now
- How does God want people to receive his message?
- How does God want us to react?
- What should people do?

CHAPTER SEVEN

The Window: Looking Out

Taking it from her hand, I looked again at the mysterious photograph. All I could see were blotches of black and white with no discernible design or identifiable image. "It makes no sense. I can't figure it out," I stated matter-of-factly as I handed the picture back to Mrs. Piper, my sixth-grade Sunday school teacher.

"Take a closer look . . . and look here," she responded, tracing her finger around the large dark spot in the center.

Confident that this was a waste of time—I had already checked out the snapshot carefully and thoroughly—with doubting sigh I took the photo and looked again. It was magic! This time I could see a face, and it looked like the face of Jesus!

Isn't it amazing how our perspective can change when we focus on something else, look from a different angle, or listen to others? As in my experience with the Sunday school photograph, suddenly our eyes are opened and we see new images, or we have new insights.

Too often, however, we block the process because we think we see everything or know it all and are not open to any advice or counsel. Consider the teenage daughter who rejects Mom's advice on dating, the wife who is closed to her husband's comments about her actions at the party, the salesman who only pretends to listen to customers' suggestions, the pastor who is sure that he knows better than the elders. But in the process of being cocky and defensive, we ignore or completely miss life-changing information. We fail to see the picture in the blotches.

God wants to give us insight into his will and into our lives. He wants to tell us how to live in a way that is pleasing to him. He wants us to see life's picture from his perspective. But for this to happen, we must listen to God's Word. We must be open to his counsel and direction.

That's why the third row in the Application Window is so important. It's where application takes place, where we begin to see our lives from God's perspective. In the last chapter, we looked through the Window *into* Scripture, to understand what was happening and what God was doing back *Then*. We also used the Window to see the relevance of the passage *Now*, to discover the timeless truths. To complete the process, however, we must look back and out from Scripture into our lives, answering the questions for the *Me* panes. This is the *Apply* stage from chapter 1.

This is not an easy process. It is natural to overlook or excuse our faults. In fact, it is much easier to *preach* to others what we learn from Scripture than to apply the principles to our own life. As we approach this third row, therefore, we should ask God to make us open to his Word and vulnerable to the Holy Spirit. We should also ask God for courage to actually carry out what we learn, to make the changes that he wants us to make.

Now let's look again at the Window and make the passage personal.

APPLICATION WINDOW

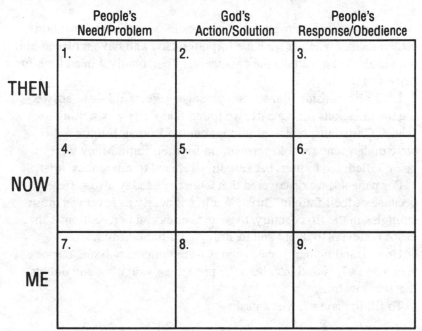

	People's Need/Problem	God's Action/Solution	People's Response/Obedience
THEN	1.	2.	3.
NOW	4.	5.	6.
ME	7.	8.	9.

The first pane in the *Me* row (#7) focuses on our specific problems or needs today. Again, I must emphasize that we should be looking for problems and needs that are parallel to those faced by the people in the passage. It will be helpful to think about all of our current pressures, temptations, struggles, and opportunities, but this particular passage will not apply to *everything* that we are facing.

Let's look again at Judges 2:10-15. In pane #1, we saw the problem: the nation of Israel, God's chosen people, had forgotten God and what he had done for them and had begun worshiping the gods of the people around them (Baal and the Ashtoreths).

Later, as we looked through pane #4, we saw that people today also take God's love and blessings for granted. They become complacent in their relationship with God. We also said that although these days people may not worship statues of wood, stone, or metal, they have other "idols" that compete for God's place in their lives. Their idols include money, possessions, abilities, pleasures, relationships, and careers.

Now, as we look closely into our lives in pane #7, we must honestly consider whether *we* have forgotten God and have replaced him with idols. We must take the passage very personally. I must look for myself in the story.

Let's also consider our second passage, 1 Peter 1:3-9. In answering the questions for pane #1, we found that Peter was writing to Jewish Christians, scattered throughout the Roman Empire, who were undergoing terrible persecution for their faith. Many were being killed, fed to lions because they refused to renounce Christ.

For pane #4, we discovered that Christians today also suffer because of their faith in Christ. While not nearly as severe as those struggles in the first century, these pressures and persecutions can cause believers to doubt and to struggle with their faith.

Understanding that persecution is a contemporary issue, our next step, pane #7, is to think about the pressures, struggles, and doubts that we now face.

To fill in pane #7, we can ask:

- How am I facing a similar problem in my life?
- How are the people in the passage like me?
- Where do I feel uneasy, a sense of conviction?

After this we move to pane #8, where we consider *God's Action or Solution* to those current problems or needs in our lives. This shouldn't be too difficult if we did a good job at pane #5. As we have seen, panes #5 and #6 describe biblical principles—truths that apply in the past, present, and future. So determining the answers for pane #8 means bringing God's action into our personal life situation, applying his solution to the problems and needs that we honestly discovered in pane #7.

To find the answers for pane #8, we can ask:

- What does God want to do in my life?
- How is God involved with me?
- What kind of person does God want me to become?

For the passage in Judges, in pane #5 we decided that God's solution to the problem of idols is that he wants people, especially his people, to love and serve *only* him. We also saw that God will use drastic means to bring his people back to him.

Clearly that principle is timeless, and it applies not just to all people but to us as well, and to me specifically. God wants *me* to love and serve him alone.

The same specific application can be seen in our second sample passage, 1 Peter 1:3-9. The principle we discovered in pane #5 is that God continues to hold out hope for all who follow him. Their eternal destiny is settled and their inheritance is sure; they will come through the trials and will be saved; they can have joy because of their faith and future hope. When I know and understand that principle, I can apply it to my specific situation of persecution. I can see how God wants to be involved with me.

At this point in the Window, we most definitely have answered the question "So what?" and are moving quickly to "Now what?" When we know the need/problem and God's action/solution, we can see what we should do about it. This last pane in the Window (#9) brings us to the action plan. This pane assumes that we know our specific need or problem (#7), God's timeless truth (panes #5 and #6), and how God wants us to respond (#8). Here we outline the specific steps we will take to obey God, to do what we know he wants us to do. This is *Doing* from chapter 1, and it is where we design an action plan. (We mentioned this in chapter 5 and will cover it thoroughly in chapter 10.)

To fill in this last pane in the Window, we can ask:

- What can I do to obey God?
- What can I do to become the kind of person God wants me to be?
- What specific steps should I take?

Answers for the idol situation might include confessing my sin to God and changing the way I spend my time and money. For the persecution problem, my first steps might include memorizing verses about the hope I have in Christ, finding a Christian friend for prayer and mutual support, and sharing my struggles with my pastor.

Of course, just writing these steps won't make them happen. I still have to actually do them. But deciding on a realistic and specific action plan will bring me very close to actually applying the Bible to my life.

SERMONS

Many pastors have found the Application Window to be a tremendous help in sermon preparation. To do this most effectively, I suggest that you prepare much as you would in personal Bible study, by working from left to right as I have explained and demonstrated in the last two chapters. But when you preach, you may want to move down the columns vertically, one pane at a time, so that you pace your application points.

Lloyd Perry, my homiletics professor at Trinity Evangelical Divinity School, recommends a sub-point of application for every main point in the sermon. In other words, don't save all the applications until the end when people are least likely to be listening because they're tired or thinking about what they have to do next. And, if you're running late, you will be tempted to condense, generalize, or skip the challenge to action. Instead, sprinkle applications throughout.

Also, consider providing tangible ways for people to respond to what they have heard God say to them through your message. This will help them actually carry out what you may suggest for panes #8 and #9. You could provide paper and pens for writing action plans, or you could include preprinted response cards in the bulletin. If the topic is compassion, in the foyer you could display two or three special projects for which members could volunteer time and money.

Obeying God means personally responding to what he tells us to do, and that involves action, not just promises. Help your listeners *do* what they know they should.

STUDYING AND DOING

Some people study, study, study and do very little about it. That would be like a football player who knows the game thoroughly and has memorized the playbook (he's tremendously knowledgeable) but who seldom practices and has never been in a game.

Others do, do, do and spend little time in study. That would be like an athlete who runs, throws, and catches footballs by the hour (he's in tremendous condition) but who spends no time learning techniques and understanding the game.

True Bible application involves both studying and doing. It means discovering what the Bible is saying to *Me* and then doing what it says. Use the Pyramid and the Application Window to help you study the Word of God and then do what it says.

WORKING IT THROUGH
Turn to Hebrews 7 again and finish working through the Application Window with the whole chapter, paragraph, or short passage that you used in chapter 6. Write the information in each pane of the *Me* row below.

APPLICATION WINDOW

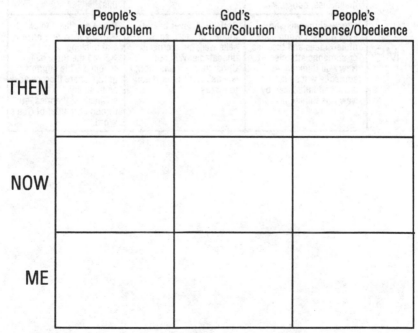

	People's Need/Problem	God's Action/Solution	People's Response/Obedience
THEN			
NOW			
ME			

Here are some possible answers for the *Me* row (I've reprinted the previous rows of the Window for your reference):

APPLICATION WINDOW

	People's Need/Problem	God's Action/Solution	People's Response/Obedience
THEN	Hebrew Christians in danger of falling back into Judaism—falling away from their faith. Why? Hard for them to accept that Christ is completely sufficient for salvation.	God used author of H. to demonstrate the superiority of Christ, how he alone is sufficient for salvation. Goes on to show Christ's credentials to be our high priest, using Melchizedek as an example.	• Persevere. • Grow and mature in their faith, study, & understand just why Christ is sufficient for salvation.
NOW	Most of us don't have an *old* religion to fall back into, but there are several *new* religions that entice us: New Age movement surrounds us, premeating all areas of our society—TV, schools, business, magazines, books, etc.	Through his Word, authors, & preachers, God is demonstrating the superiority of Jesus Christ over all religions. We must communicate this clearly & convincingly.	• Persevere. • Don't get sidetracked; don't get away from reading the Bible and searching out its truths. • Don't water down its message by accommodating faith to New Age thinking.
ME	I know someone who lives on the cutting edge of new ideas and theories, or someone attracted to New Age thinking, or someone whose faith is weak and influenced by New Age thinking.	Christ will never be outmoded or replaced. New sells well, but eternal is unbeatable. Without Christ as my foundation, I will be swept from theory to theory.	• Use my head, think. • Study New Age errors and thinking. • Read the Bible daily. • Join a Bible support group where there is accountability. • Check all theories, etc., through the filter of God's Word.

Chapter at a Glance

People's Need/Problem—Me

- How am I facing a similar problem in my life?
- How are the people in the passage like me?
- Where do I feel uneasy, a sense of conviction?

God's Action/Solution—Me

- What does God want to do in my life?
- How is God involved with me?
- What kind of person does God want me to become?

People's Response/Obedience—Me

- What can I do to obey God?
- What can I do to become the kind of person God wants me to be?
- What specific steps should I take?

APPLICATION WINDOW

	People's Need/Problem	God's Action/Solution	People's Response/Obedience
THEN	• Who needed help? • What was going on? • What was the problem?	• How did God react? • What did God do? • What did God want the people to do?	• How did the people receive God's message? • How did the people respond to God's solution? • How did God want the people to respond?
NOW	• With whom in the passage do I identify? • What tension, need, conflict, or problem sounds familiar? • How are the people in the story like us, like me?	• What is God's answer to this question today? • What is God's solution to our problem? • What is God doing now?	• How does God want people to receive his message? • How does God want us to react? • What should people do?
ME	• How am I facing a similar problem in my life? • How are the people in the passage like me? • Where do I feel uneasy, a sense of conviction?	• What does God want to do in my life? • How is God involved with me? • What kind of person does God want me to become?	• What can I do to do what God wants me to do? • What can I do to become the kind of person God wants me to be? • What specific steps should I take?

An Application Window to photocopy

APPLICATION WINDOW

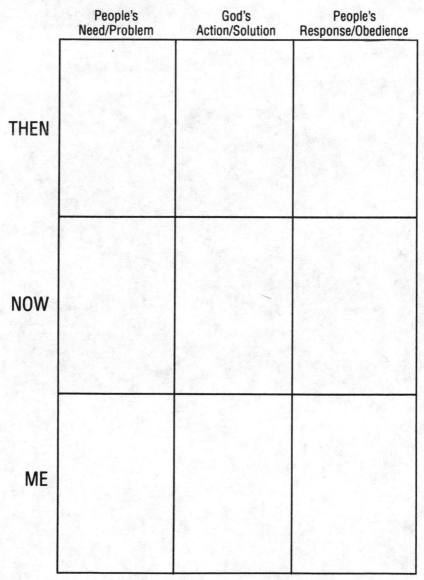

	People's Need/Problem	God's Action/Solution	People's Response/Obedience
THEN			
NOW			
ME			

CHAPTER EIGHT
Digging In: Old Testament

Tim slowly sipped his coffee as he listened to my animated description of our latest publishing venture, the proposed *Life Application Bible*. My associates and I were about to begin work on this exciting project, and I wanted Tim to share my enthusiasm. He listened patiently, nodding and smiling at appropriate moments.

"Well, what do you think?" I paused and waited for his reaction.

Slowly Tim put down the cup. Trying to be kind, but with a skeptical tone, he replied, "An application Bible sounds great. But how can you find application in every part of the Bible, especially the Old Testament? For example, I just finished reading Ezekiel and can't think of anything in there that applies. And what about Leviticus, Ecclesiastes, Obadiah, or Malachi?"

I had to admit that Tim had a good point. When you read a passage in James, such as, "Dear brothers, don't ever forget that it is best to listen much, speak little, and not become angry" (James 1:19), the application seems obvious: we should listen carefully before we speak, making sure to have all the facts in a specific situation. Not only could we apply that verse personally, we could preach it, easily stirring in two or three poignant illustrations.

On the other hand, how should we handle the genealogies, prophecies, poems, and apocalyptic visions? In those passages the applications don't tend to leap out of the text and into our lives. But if it is true that "the whole Bible was given to us by inspiration from God and is useful to teach us what is true and to make us realize what is wrong in our lives; it straightens us out and helps us do what is right" (2 Timothy 3:16), then every passage should lend itself to application. Right?

That's what the next two chapters are about—how to find applications in every part of the Bible.

Before we dig in, it's important to understand that the Bible is an anthology or a library. Although contained in one large volume, the Bible actually is a collection of sixty-six smaller books, containing a wide variety of literature. In the Bible we find dynamic prophetic declarations, emotional poetic expressions, sweeping historical narratives, deeply personal correspondence, and intricate legal delineations. And each type of literature has unique application possibilities. Let's take a closer look.

The Bible can be divided into seven literary types: Law, History, Poetry and Wisdom Literature, Prophecy, Gospels, Epistles, and Apocalypse. We will look at these types one at a time, giving application principles, suggestions, and illustrations for each one. In this chapter, we'll cover the Old Testament.

LAW

Traditionally, the five books of the Law (also known as the Pentateuch) are placed at the beginning of the Bible: Genesis, Exodus, Leviticus, Numbers, and Deuteronomy. Although these books contain historical narratives, much of the text is devoted to specific laws and regulations for the nation of Israel, the people of God. Three types of laws are included: civil law, ceremonial law, and moral law.

Civil laws were given specifically for Israel to help them organize, mobilize, and survive as a nation. These laws governed Israel's daily living. For example, Deuteronomy 24:10-11 states: "If you lend anything to another man, you must not enter his house to get his security. Stand outside! The owner will bring it out to you." Laws about money, relationships, sickness, legal proceedings, and diet belong in this category. Because our culture and society are radically different, many of these guidelines cannot be followed specifically. But we should look for the principles behind the commands as guides for our conduct.

Ceremonial laws were given to describe and guide worship, with specific instructions for the tabernacle, temple, sacrifices, and offerings. Leviticus 1:10-11 says, "If the animal used as a burnt offering is a sheep or a goat, it too must be a male, and without any blemishes. The man who brings it will kill it before the Lord on the north side of the altar, and Aaron's sons, the priests, will sprinkle its blood back and forth upon the altar." Ceremonial laws dealt with the relationship of sinful people with a holy God—every aspect of the ceremony was important and had a symbolic meaning.

Because the sacrifices were fulfilled in Christ, the final and ultimate sacrifice for sin, the ceremonial laws were no longer necessary after Jesus' death and resurrection. Although we are not bound by ceremonial laws today, the principles behind them still apply.

In contrast to the civil and ceremonial laws, the *moral laws* are God's rules for life, and they transcend culture and time. These laws are summarized in the Ten Commandments; for example, "You must not commit adultery" (Exodus 20:14).

Although we may have some questions about the Ten Commandments (for example, What is the "Sabbath" today?), the moral laws are not difficult to apply. "You must not commit adultery" is a straightforward statement of how God wants us to act.

Here are three ways to apply the other sections of the Law:

● *The Laws as Principles.* As a law is stated and case studies are described, we can look for the principle behind the law. Then we can apply that principle to our lives today.

Leviticus 5:4 states: "If anyone makes a rash vow, whether the vow is good or bad, when he realizes what a foolish vow he has taken, he is guilty." The principle behind this law is that we should be wise and self-controlled, not promising what we cannot do or what would be wrong to do.

Numbers 15:27-31 discusses the difference between sinning unintentionally and sinning defiantly, and the consequences of each action. The principle is that God is willing to forgive people who make unintentional mistakes if they realize that what they have done is wrong and change their ways. But those who sin defiantly will receive much harsher punishment. God considers both the attitude and the act.

● *Biographies: Personal Examples.* Although they lived many centuries ago in a culture far different from ours, biblical people give us a wonderful supply of examples to follow or avoid.

Numbers 16 tells the story of Korah, a priest who led a rebellion against Moses. Korah is an example of someone with many significant abilities and responsibilities but whose ambition caused him to lose everything. An application principle from this passage is to guard against ambition and greed.

● *Israel's Development Paralleling Our Spiritual Growth.* We learn in 1 Corinthians 10:1-11 that what happened to Israel occurred as examples and warnings for us. We can learn, for instance, from the constant grumbling of the children of Israel during their wilderness wanderings, their continual slipping back into idolatry, and their lack of trust. As individuals and as the church, we shouldn't repeat their mistakes.

HISTORY

In addition to portions of the Pentateuch, the historical books include Joshua, Judges, Ruth, 1 Samuel, 2 Samuel, 1 Kings, 2 Kings, 1 Chronicles, 2 Chronicles, Ezra, Nehemiah, Esther, and Acts. (Although Matthew, Mark, Luke, and John also record history, they form a separate type.)

The historian's main purpose was to record facts about events and people, not to teach religious concepts. We must be careful, therefore, not to read "teachings" into the narratives. But God inspired the writers of the Bible, so biblical history is packed with spiritual truth.

Here are three ways to find applications in the historical books.

● *Negative Examples.* As mentioned under "Law," we can learn much from biographies and stories of biblical personalities. We can read and observe how people responded to temptation, pressure, success, persecution, failure, and disaster, and how they related to God, family members, leaders, friends, coworkers, and enemies.

Many of these examples are negative. Hophni and Phinehas illustrate the results of greed and blatant disobedience (1 Samuel 4); Saul exemplifies a person consumed by pride and self-sufficiency (1 Samuel 15–31); Ahaz shows what happens to those who are involved in idolatry (2 Chronicles 28).

It is helpful to ask, Why did God put this story in the Bible? What can I learn from it?

● *Positive Examples.* We can also emulate the positive examples of many historical figures. Esther was a courageous person who took advantage of her God-given opportunities. Joshua and Nehemiah provide outstanding examples of leadership.

We shouldn't underestimate what we can learn from these stories and lives. It's easy to discount these people if we first learned about them in Sunday school or have heard the stories many times over . . . David and Goliath, Daniel in the lions' den, and Jonah and the big fish. We should dig deeper than just knowing facts.

● *Cycles of Sin and Obedience.* The historical books provide us with a panoramic view of God's work and God's people, putting events into perspective and bringing trends and cycles into view.

The book of Judges, for example, shows that during prosperity, the people of Israel would grow complacent and self-sufficient, eventually forgetting God and rebelling against him. Then God would punish the nation by allowing the people to be conquered by enemy nations. The people would respond by repenting and crying out to God for help. In his love and mercy, God would raise up a judge who would deliver the children of Israel from their enemies. Then the people would remain loyal to God under the leadership of that judge. But when the judge died, the people would forget God and slip back into sin, and the cycle would begin again.

These cycles are also repeated with the kings and in individual lives. And there are lessons for us at each turn of the cycle. We can gain perspective on our spiritual cycles, in our personal relationship with God, and in our families, churches, and nation.

Acts is a New Testament historical book, recording the history of the early church. The same principles of interpretation apply to Acts as to the other historical books. In addition, because we are part of Christ's church, we can watch the young church in action and glean lessons for our lives.

POETRY

The poems and Wisdom Literature (Job, Psalms, Proverbs, Ecclesiastes, and Song of Solomon) are quite varied and form a beautiful and large portion of the Bible with innumerable implications for our worship and lifestyle. It should be noted that most prophecy was also recorded in poetic form. Isaiah is the most obvious example of this.

To find and apply the messages in these books, consider the following categories.

● *Practical Wisdom.* The wisdom books provide just that—wisdom, insights and guidelines for living. Proverbs, for example, tells us about people who have wisdom and enjoy its benefits. A *proverb* is a short, wise, easy-to-learn saying that calls a person to action. It doesn't argue about basic spiritual and moral beliefs but assumes that we already hold them.

Proverbs are not laws or moral absolutes. Rather, they are catchy, short statements that express practical truisms. They express common sense that focuses on God—his character, works, and blessings—and how we can live in close relationship to him.

Consider, for example, the following statements: "If you are looking for advice, stay away from fools" (Proverbs 14:7); "Discipline your son and he will give you happiness and peace of mind" (Proverbs 29:17); "Two can accomplish more than twice as much as one, for the results can be much better. If one falls, the other pulls him up; but if a man falls when he is alone, he's in trouble" (Ecclesiastes 4:9-10).

You'll find nuggets of practical wisdom sprinkled throughout this section of the Old Testament.

● *Worship.* In the Psalms, David and the other writers expressed their praise and adoration for God. "O Lord our God, the majesty and glory of your name fills all the earth and overflows the heavens. You have taught the little children to praise you perfectly. May their example shame and silence your enemies!" (Psalm 8:1-2).

The profound and deep expressions of the Psalms can teach us how to open ourselves to God, how to pray, and how to worship. Many people worship by singing or praying these beautiful poems of love and devotion.

● *Attributes of God.* The poems and Wisdom Literature also tell us much about what God is like. Read Job 38–41 and you will gain a fresh appreciation for God's majesty and might. Who can read Song of Solomon and not sense God's kind of love? The more we know about God, the more our lives will change as we seek to glorify, honor, and obey him.

PROPHECY

Next we come to the prophetic books. The office of prophet was instituted during the days of Samuel, who was the last judge. Along with the priests, prophets were God's special representatives. Their role was to be God's spokespersons, confronting national leaders and the people with God's commands and promises. When the word *prophet* is mentioned, we usually think of people of God foretelling the future. But the prophets' main task was to *forth*tell God's messages, whatever it happened to be—to proclaim his word. The prophetic books tell the stories of these prophets and retell their pronouncements.

Applications from the prophetic books can be discovered by remembering the following:

● *The Prophet's Role.* In addition to hearing the prophets' messages, we can learn from the prophets by checking out their lives. Isaiah and Ezekiel spoke and *lived* their prophetic messages, often enduring tremendous hardship (see Isaiah 6 and 20 and Ezekiel 4, 12, and 24). Jeremiah's heart was broken over the message he had to deliver. Amos was a layman, a businessman, called from the fields. And Hosea, his wife, and his children became living object lessons of God's truth. Hundreds of lessons shout to us from their lives, perhaps the most obvious being that we also should have courage to speak out for God.

● *The Character of God.* Because the prophets spoke for God, we can see God in action as he related to them. We also can learn about God's character by studying the prophets' public pronouncements. God's holiness, righteousness, grace, justice, and love are a few of the attributes that come to mind. We worship, serve, and obey the same God today.

● *Social Action.* In addition to the sweeping condemnations of idolatry, judgments on sin, and calls to righteous living, the prophetic books also contain numerous references to specific social ills and remedies—caring for the poor, feeding the hungry, freeing the oppressed. Our world still has multitudes of poor, hungry, and oppressed people. There are innumerable social situations that are sinful. And God's Word still applies.

Think of the contemporary nations and individuals to whom this prophecy could apply: "The people of Israel have sinned again and again, and I will not forget it. I will not leave them unpunished any more. For they have perverted justice by accepting bribes, and sold into slavery the poor who can't repay their debts; they trade them for a pair of shoes. They trample the poor in the dust and kick aside the meek" (Amos 2:6-7).

Reading the prophets can and should be a life-changing experience.

Of course, during my brief conversation with Tim in that restaurant many years ago I did not explain all of the principles outlined above. In fact, to be perfectly honest, his question raised doubts in my mind about the whole project and about Bible application. But since then I've learned, through study and from personal experience, that the whole Bible is packed with lessons for our lives . . . even the Old Testament!*

---

*For a chart that summarizes chapters 8 and 9, see Appendix D, "Applying Each Type of Bible Literature" (pages 153–165).

WORKING IT THROUGH

Find a biblical principle, a timeless truth, in each of the following passages:

1. *Law*—Leviticus 25:35-37

2. *History*—1 Kings 3:6-9

3. *Poetry*—Psalm 144:3-4

4. *Wisdom Literature*—Proverbs 28:4

5. *Prophecy*—Isaiah 29:13-14

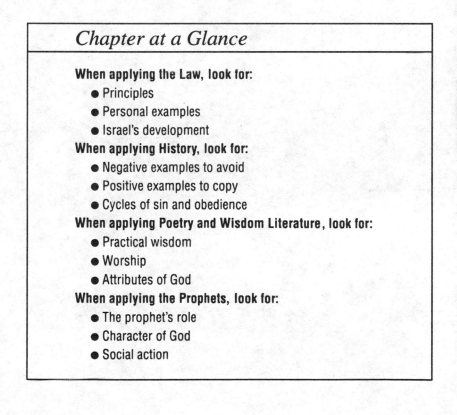

Chapter at a Glance

When applying the Law, look for:
- Principles
- Personal examples
- Israel's development

When applying History, look for:
- Negative examples to avoid
- Positive examples to copy
- Cycles of sin and obedience

When applying Poetry and Wisdom Literature, look for:
- Practical wisdom
- Worship
- Attributes of God

When applying the Prophets, look for:
- The prophet's role
- Character of God
- Social action

CHAPTER NINE
Digging In: New Testament

New! Improved! The latest! Fresh! Now!

Those adjectives imply that products, services, programs, or information is current and up-to-date. They are used in advertising to attract customers, pique interest, and make sales. After all, old is all right for history buffs or antiques, but no one wants to be out of style, out of date, passé . . . right?

Many people carry that attitude into their Bible study, seeing the *Old* Testament as old, dusty, ancient history that is out of touch. But the New Testament is different, they think. After all, it's "new" . . . or at least newer.

In some ways they are right—the New Testament was written after the Old Testament, so it is more recent. But to think that way about *Old* and *New* is to have a very shallow and superficial view of Scripture. As we have seen with many examples throughout this book and especially in the previous chapter, the Old Testament is very much up-to-date and relevant to our lives. The biblical principles from Genesis 1 through Malachi 4 are *timeless*—important to know and apply. God inspired *all* Scripture, so we should study all of it to discover his guidance and will. It would be a terrible mistake to relegate the Old Testament to the dusty shelf of irrelevance.

The New Testament is not called "new" because it *replaces* the Old Testament or because it was written more recently. Rather it is "new" because it *fulfills* the "old." The Bible is the story of God and his relationship with humankind and with his own people. This is a loving God, a covenant God, who promises to send a Savior. His promises from the Old Testament are filled in the New Testament.

- What the priests pictured in the Old Testament is fulfilled in the New.
- What the prophets predicted in the Old Testament comes to pass in the New.
- What God promised in the Old Testament happens in the New.

Actually, the two Testaments fit together and must be understood together. The Old prepares the way for the New, and the New interprets the Old. We can't fully understand what God intended in the Old Testament without a knowledge of the New. And we can't fully understand the New Testament without a knowledge of the Old.

So as we come to the New Testament, the story of Christ and the church, don't think of it as "God's Word, new and improved." Rather, approach this collection of books as "God's Word, the rest of the story."

The New Testament contains three literary types: History—the Gospels and Acts (covered in chapter 8), the Epistles, and the Apocalypse. The New Testament books are also arranged in that order in our Bibles. Matthew and the other Gospels tell the story of Jesus Christ; Acts chronicles the growth of the church; the letters of Paul, the writer of Hebrews, James, Peter, and John teach doctrine, give guidance, and solve problems for those early believers; and then Revelation (the Apocalypse) closes with a prophetic vision of hope and triumph.

GOSPELS

The four Gospels (Matthew, Mark, Luke, and John) are biographies of Jesus, written by eyewitnesses and historians. Because these are historical books, the application categories discussed in the section on "history" (in chapter 8) are relevant. We can, for example, learn much from looking at the lives of Mary, John the Baptist, the disciples, and other characters.

The Gospels form a separate division, however, because they are His-story—they tell us about Jesus, the Messiah, the Son of God.

In studying the life of Christ, there are several areas where we can find applications.

● *Jesus' Lifestyle.* Jesus told his disciples that if they wanted to know what God was like, they should look at him (John 14:9). Do you want to see God in action, in the flesh? Look at Christ.

We are also told that the goal of the Christian life is to be like Christ (Romans 8:29). It only makes sense, then, to use his lifestyle as our example and model. How did Jesus evangelize? Relate to sinners, the poor, the sick, and the oppressed? Teach the disciples? Obey his Father? Defeat temptation? Deal with hypocrisy? Asking questions like these can teach us how we should act.

Mark 1:40-45 records the story of Jesus healing a leper. Verses 41-42 state: "And Jesus, moved with pity, touched him [the leper] and said, 'I want to! Be healed!' Immediately the leprosy was gone—the man was healed!" Two lessons from Jesus' lifestyle jump out at me from this passage: his compassion for hurting people ("moved with pity") and the fact that he touched the leper (an unclean, outcast, and "untouchable" person in that society). When I consider my lack of compassion for the needy in my community and the fact that I take great pains to avoid touching "dirty" people, I am convicted. I need to follow Christ's example.

● *Ethical Teachings.* Often Jesus gave specific statements about how people, especially his followers, were to live. Twenty centuries later, we still follow him, so those statements also apply to us. Check out the Sermon on the Mount (Matthew 5–7) and the Upper Room Discourse (John 13–17). We could spend months studying, learning, and applying just those sections.

In John 16:33, we find a strong word of encouragement from Jesus to his disciples: "I have told you all this so that you will have peace of heart and mind. Here on earth you will have many trials and sorrows; but cheer up, for I have overcome the world." Christ's teaching for me is clear: as a human being in a fallen world, I will encounter difficulties and struggles, and as a follower of Christ, I will be pressured and tested. But regardless of the problems, I can have hope because I have Christ.

● *Parables.* When Jesus spoke to the gathered multitudes, he often used parables—stories with a message. Later he would explain the meaning of the parable to his disciples. These interesting stories contain principles for us, but we should be careful not to read too much into them. Usually there is one main point that Jesus is making. If there are more, he says so. When studying the parables, we should consider Jesus' explanation and the context to discover the timeless truth. Then we can bring that principle into our current situations.

The parable of the four soils, for example, can teach us much about how people respond to the Word of God (see Luke 8:4-15). But we shouldn't try to find a special meaning for every part of the story such as the path, birds, rocks, etc.

The parable of the wealthy fool is in Luke 12:16-21. In this story, the rich man had such an abundance of crops that he planned to tear down his barns and build bigger ones. He thought, "I'll sit back and say to myself, 'Friend, you have enough stored away for years to come. Now take it easy! Wine, women, and song for you!'" (verse 19). But that night the man would die. Jesus ended this parable by explaining, "Every man is a fool who gets rich on earth but not in heaven" (verse 21). Every time I read or hear that parable, I am reminded to keep my values and priorities straight. Earthly treasures are worthless when seen in the light of eternity.

● *Figures of Speech.* Another gold mine of applications is the collection of word pictures and metaphors that Jesus used to describe himself and his kingdom. Jesus said he was "bread" (John 6:35), "the light" (John 8:12), a "gate" (John 10:7), and "the true Vine" (John 15:1). And the kingdom of God is described as seeds and weeds, a mustard seed, a woman making bread, hidden treasure, a pearl merchant, and a net (see Matthew 13). How is Christ your bread? What are the "weeds" in your life?

EPISTLES

Many of the New Testament books are formal letters (also called epistles), written by Paul and others to local churches and individuals. These are usually seen as the easiest Bible books to apply, but even here it is helpful to consider certain application categories.

● *Doctrines.* As the early church was being established, Paul and the other disciples spent much time defining and explaining theology to new believers. Questions about the nature of God, guilt and forgiveness, law and grace, eternal destiny, and so forth needed to be answered. Knowing these doctrines is vital for any growing Christian. But we must go beyond being correct and knowing the facts. We must allow these truths to permeate and change our lives.

Consider, for example, the personal implications of such doctrines as the sovereignty of God, the priesthood of believers, the reality of heaven and hell, and the ministry of the Holy Spirit.

In Romans 8:1-17, Paul explains the freedom that is ours in Christ, how Christ frees us from the "vicious circle of sin and death" (verse 2). As we read this passage, we discover that although we will always have a sin nature to contend with, we don't have to be controlled by it. Christ gives us the power through his Holy Spirit to do what is right, to "behave like God's very own children" (verse 15). The secret is in our will, where we yield ourselves and change our behavior.

That theological message is intensely practical. We don't *have to* do what is sinful and harmful. Through the power of the Holy Spirit, we can do what is pleasing to God.

● *Ethics.* The Epistles also contain many direct statements about how we should act. In Galatians 6:3-5 we read: "If anyone thinks he is too great to stoop to this, he is fooling himself. He is really a nobody. Let everyone be sure that he is doing his very best, for then he will have the personal satisfaction of work well done, and won't need to compare himself with someone else. Each of us must bear some faults and burdens of his own. For none of us is perfect!"

The applications from these verses and most of the other ethical passages are relatively easy to determine. It is important, however, to understand the historical context in which these instructions were written. For more on this, you can review the discussion in chapter 4, under *People, Place,* and *Plot.*

● *Church Conflicts*. Often the occasion for writing a letter was a church conflict, whether it was the problem of eating meat that had been offered to idols (Romans 14), believers taking each other to court (1 Corinthians 6), a quarrel between two women (Philippians 4:2), or another pressing issue. After understanding the culture and the conflict, we can discover the relevant principle. We can also learn from watching how Paul and other church leaders resolved their conflicts.

The letter to Philemon gives a wonderful example of how to resolve a potential interpersonal conflict in the church. Onesimus was a runaway slave who ran to Rome and there came to faith in Christ through Paul's ministry. Paul wrote this letter to Onesimus's master, Philemon, asking him to treat his former slave as a "brother in Christ" (verse 16). Although we don't have slaves today, we can find many lessons for our lives by seeing how Paul related to both Onesimus and Philemon and the style and spirit of his inspired letter.

APOCALYPSE

Although apocalyptic literature (dramatic and violent prophesies of the future) can also be found in Isaiah, Ezekiel, Daniel, and Zechariah, the title *Apocalypse* is reserved for the book of Revelation, where John records his God-given vision of the future. In many ways, everything we discussed about prophecy also applies here; but Revelation is unique as a New Testament prophetic book—it is a separate type.

When studying Revelation, we should remember these themes:

● *The Church*. The first three chapters are messages to specific first-century churches in Asia, but they are typical of churches and believers throughout the centuries. Reading God's messages to these churches can give us insight and direction in our own church setting.

For example, in Christ's message to the church at Laodicea (Revelation 3:14-22), he condemns the people for being lukewarm—neither hot nor cold in their love for God. The Laodicean church was rich, but their wealth had made them self-sufficient and indifferent to God. This message could be read again and again in many churches today. Wealthy, with beautiful sanctuaries, multiple staff, and multi-faceted programs, modern churches are often self-centered and spiritually dead. May we heed Christ's warnings in Revelation!

● *Hope.* The first readers of this book were oppressed believers, many of whom were facing torture and death because of their faith. Revelation was a message of hope for them. How are we in a similar situation? How can this book give us hope?

Think of what the first-century readers must have felt when they read about the "souls of those who had been martyred for preaching the Word of God and for being faithful in their witnessing" (6:9) and who called loudly to the Lord, "O Sovereign Lord, holy and true, how long will it be before you judge the people of the earth for what they've done to us? When will you avenge our blood against those living on the earth?" (6:10)

Those early believers were undergoing terrible persecution for their faith and had seen many friends and loved ones tortured and killed. Knowing that God understood their plight and that his justice would eventually triumph must have been a great comfort and encouragement.

Although we may not suffer such severe persecution, God's message in Revelation can also give us hope when we are ridiculed or discriminated against because of our faith. We can continue to serve God with joy, knowing that what we believe is right and true.

● *Judgment and Victory.* Beyond the past and the present, Revelation gives many future predictions of conflict, oppression, war, and Christ's ultimate victory, the climax of history. What implications do these events have for us? They should motivate us to be faithful and to be prepared for Christ's return.

In the next to last verse in Revelation, Jesus says, "He who has said all these things declares: Yes, I am coming soon!" Then John responds, "Amen! Come, Lord Jesus!" John welcomed and longed for Christ's return. He was ready. As I read that verse, I wonder about my readiness. If Jesus were to come back today, would I be prepared? Do I have that same longing in my heart for Christ's return? What should I do to be ready?

The *whole* Bible is God's Word to us—Old Testament and New. May we faithfully dig in and dig out his truth for our lives.

WORKING IT THROUGH
Find a biblical principle, a timeless truth, in each of the following passages:

1. *Gospels*—Matthew 6:1-4; Luke 7:18-35; John 10:1-21

2. *Epistles*—1 Corinthians 10:12-13; Hebrews 2:16-18; 1 John 3:17-20

3. *Apocalypse*—Revelation 2:1-7; Revelation 19:1-10

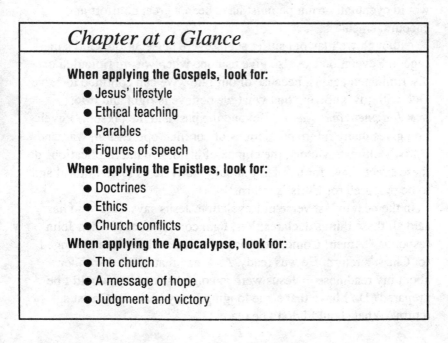

Chapter at a Glance

When applying the Gospels, look for:
- Jesus' lifestyle
- Ethical teaching
- Parables
- Figures of speech

When applying the Epistles, look for:
- Doctrines
- Ethics
- Church conflicts

When applying the Apocalypse, look for:
- The church
- A message of hope
- Judgment and victory

PART THREE
Making Applications

CHAPTER TEN

Design an Action Plan

"All right, guys, listen up!" Quiet filled the crowded locker room as the coach turned and faced his team. "This is our first game and our first challenge." Coach slowly turned his head as he spoke, looking each young man in the eye. He continued with a whispered intensity and short, choppy sentences. "The Raiders are good. But we can beat this team. We're in better shape. We have better athletes. We have better equipment. We have better fans. And we want it more!" Then he shouted, "Am I right?"

"Yes!" came the deafening response, as in unison the players raised their helmets and voices.

"Do you want it?"

"Yes!" they roared back again.

"Put those helmets on!" Clicks of snapped chin straps echoed throughout the room. "Now stand and circle." Thirty-five young athletes circled their coach, each straining to get close, hands reaching to the center of the circle.

Then the captains began to chant, "Win, win, win." Louder and louder it grew to a deafening peak. Then the coach yelled, *"Now!"*

The players rushed from the locker room and poured onto the field.

Sixty minutes of football later, the players sat in that same room in silence. They were dirty, tired, beat up . . . defeated.

On paper, they should have won. Their team really *did* have superior equipment and players. And they were highly motivated—they "wanted it bad." But they lost because they were missing a vital ingredient—a game plan, a strategy.

Now shifting the scene from the football field to the field of life, let's assume that you are in condition, in great spiritual shape. That is, you are close to God and have worked hard at understanding how to study the Bible and how to dig out its timeless truths. Let's also assume that you have mastered the Bible study skills—you know how to use the Pyramid and Window and are very good at it. Finally, let's assume that you are highly motivated; in other words, you *want* to hear God speaking through his Word and then apply it to your life. The truth is that unless you have a game plan, a strategy for actually doing what you have learned, life-changing application probably will not occur.

In chapter 1, I said the last step in the Bible study process is *Do*. That means designing an action plan, obeying God and putting into practice what he has taught us in his Word, knowing what God wants us to be and do *Now*. The step before, *Apply,* answers the question "So what?" The *Do* step answers "Now what?"

In chapter 5, I explained that the *Plan* step in the Bible study Pyramid is where we put truth into practice by determining to change and then making plans to live differently. To help us plan, we can ask:

- What does God want me to *do* about what I have learned?
- What steps will get me to that goal?
- What should be my first step? How can I get started?

SETTING THE GOAL

Before we can design a strategy for change we first must determine a goal. Remember your last family vacation? You had a goal—you knew where you wanted to arrive. Without that destination, or goal, you could have had a pleasant drive with the family, but you wouldn't have gotten anywhere. Goals can be long or short, quantitative or qualitative, general or specific. For example, your goal may have been to drive to San Francisco (from Chicago); it may have been to visit Grandma at her house an hour away; or it may have been to take a scenic drive through Wisconsin and then return home. Whatever the case, you need a goal—then you can determine a strategy for getting from here to there.

In Bible study, the goals emerge in the *Apply* section. Here's how it works with the Bible study Pyramid.

As you study God's Word and discover his *Principles* (at the peak of the Application Pyramid), the Holy Spirit will begin to convict you about certain areas in your life. Then as you work through the *Present, Parallels,* and *Priorities* steps, you will begin to realize the specific changes that you need to make. For example, when studying James 3, you may be convicted about your speech, the use of your tongue. You understand that the principle is that Christians should watch what they say and use their tongues to praise God, not to curse people. Thinking through your present situation and looking for various parallels in your life, you remember that after church last Sunday, you were very critical of the worship service, especially the pastor's sermon. You decide that God is telling you to confess your critical spirit to him, to stop cutting down the pastor, and to develop a positive attitude toward your church. Those are your goals.

Application goals don't always have to focus on *doing*—stopping certain actions or starting others. A goal can involve *being*—developing character, changing priorities, becoming closer to God, being Christlike, and so forth. In either case, you should try to make the application goal as specific as possible. For example, instead of determining to "be a more loving person," a better goal would be to be more loving in a certain relationship. Or, instead of deciding to be a stronger witness for Christ, a more realistic and reachable goal would be to be a better witness for Christ in a specific relationship or circumstance, such as *at work.* A goal is *where you want to be.*

After determining your goal, you are ready to design a plan to reach that goal.

DESIGNING THE PLAN

As I mentioned in chapter 5, there are two types of plans: *intentional* and *conditional.* Intentional plans are step-by-step guides for taking action. Conditional plans, however, are anticipated responses to situations that might arise, and they usually follow an "If . . . , then . . ." format. In other words, *If* this occurs, *then* I will respond by acting this way."

Conditional Plans. Intentional plans are easier to use because they are concrete, specific, and measurable. But some application goals can only be reached through conditional plans.

Take, for example, the whole area of temptation. If a person is not presently in a tempting situation, then he or she will need a conditional plan to meet the application goal of resisting a specific temptation: "If I am offered a marijuana cigarette, then I will refuse." "If the conversation turns to gossip, then I will politely excuse myself and walk away." "If the cashier gives me too much change, then I will tell him or her about the mistake and give the money back."

Relationship issues are also prime candidates for conditional plans. A parent who decides to respond quietly but firmly to his child's disobedience may have to decide, "If Jon throws a tantrum, then I will explain his punishment and carry it out without losing my temper and screaming." A Christian high school student who has determined not to date non-Christians may need to say, "If I am asked out by a non-Christian, then I will politely decline." A store clerk may decide, *If the boss asks me to work on Sunday, I will explain that I don't want to because of my religious convictions.*

Conditional plans can be very helpful. It's much better to think through how you should and want to act in a specific situation *before* it occurs than to suddenly be thrust into it. So don't assume that just because you haven't yet experienced a specific temptation or pressure you can't design an action plan; a conditional plan will work just fine.

Intentional Plans. In contrast, intentional plans are very specific and action oriented. There's nothing especially spiritual about these plans. We use them to accomplish all sorts of goals, everything from losing weight to having a beautiful lawn.

Intentional plans contain action steps within the individual's control. An intentional plan might have the statement, "I will" followed by a To Do list in chronological order (a "1 . . . 2 . . . 3 . . ." format).

It will be helpful to visualize intentional plans as a set of stairs. At the top step is the goal; the other stairs are steps to reach that goal.

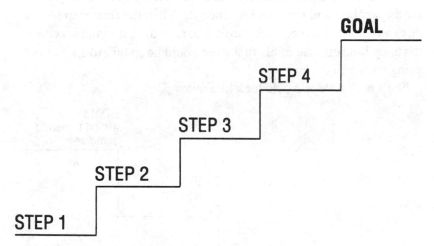

It's important to keep these steps small and manageable. Think of yourself as a small child. You are standing at the foot of the stairs at the front of your house, and you want to get something off the front porch. If the steps are each a foot high and you are only about two feet tall, you won't be able to get to the porch. Often we do this with our goals, and so we never take that first step.

Suppose Ted reads in 1 Samuel 2:27-36 about Eli and his self-centered sons, Hophni and Phinehas. Ted sees Eli as a bad example of a father, and he is convicted about his fathering role and decides to be a godly father. That goal is so big, it would take two stories of stairs to get there. Ted needs to think of a realistic and specific goal. At this point, however, Ted doesn't have a clue as to how to do that or where to start. But instead of giving up, he decides to attend a seminar on Christian fathering. Now that's a much more realistic and reachable goal. But even here, if Ted's not careful, he can make this step so steep that he will give up trying to climb the stairs. He could, for example, make his first step "Sign up for a seminar," without having a clue about where or when this kind of seminar is offered.

A much better first step would be to call the pastor and ask about seminars or for leads on where he can get information. The next step would be to call for a brochure. The third step would be to register for the seminar and put it on his schedule. Then the final step would be to attend. If Ted feels awkward about attending a seminar across town, by himself, one of his first steps could be to talk to Jack about going with him.

Ted's action steps would look like this:

```
                                              GOAL:
                                              attend fathering
                                              seminar
                                             ┌─────────

                              STEP 3:
                              register for
                              seminar
                             ┌─────────

               STEP 2:
               call for seminar
               brochure
              ┌─────────

STEP 1:
call pastor about
seminar
┌─────────
```

I can hear the wheels turning: you are thinking, "That's so simple, so elementary. I would take steps like that without thinking. What's the big deal about working this through? And why should I write it down?"

Good questions. But if it's so easy, why do we have such a difficult time doing what we know God wants us to do? Why do we make such slow progress in the Christian life? Why do we see so little change in our lives?

My point? It's not easy. It's simple, but it's not easy, especially when

God speaks to us about an ingrained habit, a lifestyle, or a change in priorities. Recently an accountant told me that he continues to be amazed at the small amounts of money that Christians give to God's work. He knows because he does a lot of tax returns for Christians. According to recent studies, evangelical Christians give an average of 3 percent of their income. I am sure that many of these folks have been convicted a time or two about their level of giving—while reading the Bible, hearing a sermon, or listening to a tape, they felt guilty and thought something like *I ought to do more. I need to get my giving up to at least 10 percent.* And they may even start supporting a Youth for Christ worker or a missionary for ten dollars a month and give more in the offering plate the next Sunday. But without a plan, their good intentions stop right there, and they never reach their goal.

Or what about having a daily quiet time, or witnessing to neighbors and coworkers, or doing something to help homeless people? I could go on and on. You need a plan to get it done.

GETTING STARTED

Even after designing a realistic action plan, you still have to overcome the biggest hurdle—inertia. The most difficult step to take is the first one. This is true with running. I can find all sorts of excuses to stay comfortable and *not* run. But if I have put on my jogging clothes, warmed up, and laced up my shoes, then I go running. It's hard to turn back once I've tied those shoes.

Here's how to overcome inertia and get going: make the first step so small that you can take it almost without trying, and so easy that you can't miss.

● After reading Romans 10:5-15, Barb felt convicted about her efforts to tell her best friend, Julie, about Christ. She decided that her goal would be to share her testimony with Julie when the opportunity arose. Barb knew that to do that she would have to think through what she would say and how to say it. She also decided to attend the adult Sunday school class on "Lifestyle Evangelism" and to read *Out of the Salt Shaker* by Becky Pippert. Those were steps in her strategy. But for her first step, Barb decided to pray for Julie every day, first thing in the morning and last thing at night. Her first step was simply to make a special card to remind her to pray.

● Daryl was reading Haggai 1 when he read the words: "'Is it a time for you yourselves to be living in your paneled houses, while this house remains a ruin?'" (verse 3, NIV) Although God was speaking about the Jews who had returned from captivity in Babylon and about the temple in Jerusalem, Daryl decided that God cares about his house of worship. For Daryl, that meant Community Church. As he thought about possible applications of this principle, Daryl decided that he should do something to fix up areas of the church building that were showing signs of wear and age. Daryl's first step was to take a walking tour of the building, writing down every area that needed cleaning, fixing, renovating, and so forth.

● In church last Sunday, the pastor's text was Galatians 3:26-29, and his topic was unity in Christ. Charmaine listened carefully—she was hit hard by the message, especially the point about Christ obliterating the divisions between the sexes, races, and cultures. Charmaine felt convicted about her relationship at work with Margaret. Charmaine knew that she had avoided Margaret because she was of a different race. And the more Charmaine thought about it, the more she became aware of her racist attitudes. She decided to try to establish a friendship with Margaret. Charmaine's first step was simply to smile and greet Margaret warmly the next day at work.

When you take the first step, you will be much more likely to achieve your goal.

SUB-STEPS

Of course you may have to have many more than three steps to reach your goal if you want to keep the steps small and manageable. In that case, think of your three steps as plateaus and then add sub-steps underneath to reach each plateau.

A number of years ago, I decided that I wanted to run a marathon. Up to that point, I was running about five miles on a regular basis. But it's a big jump from five miles to 26.2 miles! A veteran runner informed me that I needed to train three months to be ready for a

marathon, and he gave me a training schedule from a running maga-
zine. I decided on a marathon to train for and marked three months
back on the calendar.

The first step in the training schedule was quite easy: I was supposed to run three miles. Because that was less than I was already
running, I jumped right in. Actually the first two weeks weren't bad
at all. I was increasing my weekly mileage without even feeling it.
By the time I got to the difficult runs, I had invested so much that I
couldn't quit. Eventually I finished the training . . . and the marathon.

I was able to reach this seemingly out-of-reach goal because the
steps were small and manageable, especially the first one.

Tony was in a Bible study sponsored by the Gathering of Men. Each
Saturday morning they would discuss a topic that was relevant to men
and discover what the Bible had to say about it. For one month, they
discussed various aspects of being a Christian father. Tony really
enjoyed the study and the discussions. He was learning a lot about himself and the Bible. But when the leader had everyone read Deuteronomy 6:1-9 and the discussion turned to being a Christian influence in
the home, Tony began to feel guilty. He knew that he wasn't doing
nearly enough to "impress" God's commandments on his children. For
one thing, he was out of town for at least two days every week because
of his job. And when he was home, he was consumed with watching
sports on television or playing tennis at the club.

Tony wanted to be a good Christian father, but he knew he would
have to make some changes, especially in his schedule and priorities.
His goal was "to spend at least ten hours each week in activities with
the family." To reach this goal, Tony knew that he would have to
schedule his trips and tennis around the family's activities instead of
the other way around. He also would have to cut back on his television viewing and play with the kids instead. Tony also determined to
plan at least one special family activity each month. Those three
changes became his large steps or plateaus.

Tony got excited as he began to design his plan. And as he prayed
and then wrote in the sub-steps, he was sure the plan would work.
Here's the plan that Tony designed.

GOAL: Ten hours
per week with
family

STEP 3: One
special family
activity each month

STEP 2: Cut back
on TV and play with
kids instead.

STEP 1: Schedule
trips & tennis
around family.

His sub-steps for STEP 1 looked like this:

STEP 1: Schedule trips & tennis around family.

SUB-STEP 5:
Talk with boss
about changing
conflicting trips.

SUB-STEP 4:
Tell tennis
partner the
open days to
play.

SUB-STEP 3:
Have family
meeting to
check
schedules.

SUB-STEP 2:
Buy calendar for
family master
schedule.

SUB-STEP 1:
Discuss plan
with Marie.

Sub-steps for Tony's Step 2 could include: go to Christian bookstore to find family games to play; talk with family about having game nights instead of television on certain nights of the week; decide on maximum sporting events to watch each week.

His sub-steps for Step 3 could include: block out one day or evening a month on master calendar for special family activity; talk with wife and brainstorm possible activities with other fathers; decide on first three activities and get information on them. (I must also add that when Tony talked everything over with his wife, Marie, she was very supportive and shared that she had been praying for this for quite some time.)

You don't want to make this too complicated, but sub-steps can be very helpful in helping you reach your main steps and eventually your goal.

BOTH PLANS

As I explained in chapter 5, sometimes the application for a passage will lead to both types of plans, conditional and intentional. For example, my step-by-step or intentional plans for applying the "love" principle in 1 Corinthians 13:4-7 might be:

I will be more loving toward Gail by:
1. Not complaining when I come home from work.
2. Clearing the table after dinner.
3. Bringing her roses next week.

And my conditional plan might be:
If she has had a bad day, then I will listen to her feelings and not argue with her.

If as a result of reading in the Psalms I see that I need to praise God more, I could design an intentional plan that would include these steps:
1. List items of praise.
2. Pray through the list every morning.

3. Look up praise songs in the hymnal.
4. Lead the family in singing a praise song a week.

My conditional plan could read:
If I am cut off in traffic (usually an occasion for grumbling and shouting), then I will smile and say, "Praise the Lord."

Again, I must emphasize that when neither the conditional ("If . . . , then . . .") plan or the intentional ("1 . . . 2 . . . 3 . . .") plan seems to work for one of your applications, you probably do not yet have it clearly worked out to the level of concrete actions and should go back to *Present, Parallels,* or *Priorities.* My experience has shown that every practical application will lend itself to one of these two types of action plans.

ACCOUNTABILITY
If you are really serious about designing a plan of action and then following through on your plan, share your plan with another Christian and ask him or her to hold you accountable. This person can also give you feedback on your goals and strategies.

If you are married, your spouse can be the one to hold you accountable. But you could also choose your pastor, a counselor, a coworker, or a close Christian friend. Explain your goal and your strategy for reaching it. Ask him or her to pray for you regularly, that you would have the discipline to follow through. Also ask this person to check up on how you are doing on a regular basis. This could be at a time that you usually get together (for example, a Bible study, Sunday school class, etc.), it could be at a set time during the week to meet for coffee, or it could be a phone call. Pledge to this friend that you will give him or her an honest answer when he or she asks how it's going.

Another great place for accountability is a small group. We use Growth Groups at our church, and I would feel very comfortable sharing my goals and strategies with my group. It wouldn't be right to dominate each group meeting with my situation, but everyone would be very supportive if I were to honestly share how God was working in my life.

Holding someone accountable doesn't have to take a long time. It can be as quick as catching that person's eye, getting his or her attention, and asking, "How's it going with _____?" If the person doesn't want to talk just then or needs more time, you can explain that you will give him or her a call later.

Holding each other accountable for applying the Bible to our lives is the body of Christ in action.

To see the Bible come alive in your life, answer the question "Now what?" by writing specific goals, designing realistic plans, and finding someone to hold you accountable. "Do not merely listen to the word, and so deceive yourselves. Do what it says" (James 1:22, NIV).

WORKING IT THROUGH

Write three specific goals that God has been speaking to you about recently.

1. _____

2. _____

3. _____

Write conditional plans for the goals where necessary.

1. If _____

   then _____

2. If _____

   then _____

3. If _____

   then _____

Write a three-step intentional plan for at least one of your goals (make sure the first step is very easy to reach).

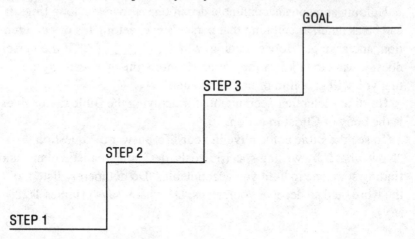

Who will you choose to hold you accountable for working your plan and reaching your goals?

CHAPTER ELEVEN

Take It Home

"You idiot!" Keri screamed at her younger sister. "Look what you did to the hair dryer. Now I'll never be ready in time."

"You kids stop fighting and hurry up," yelled Dad up the stairs. "Between you and your mother, I don't know who's slower."

"I heard that," answered Mom from the bathroom. "It's easy for you to bark orders. All you have to do is take care of yourself while I'm getting everyone else going. If you're so impatient, leave now— you can go alone!"

Five minutes later, the scowling family silently squeezed into the car, each person harboring angry, hateful, and bitter thoughts.

Then they drove to church.

Does that sound familiar? Unfortunately, it's very realistic . . . and dripping with irony—a Christian family, screaming and fighting their way to enjoy sweet fellowship, inspiring worship, and biblical teaching. It's as though what we learn from the Bible and in church makes very little difference where we live. In other words, we fail to put our faith into practice with our families.

We shouldn't be too surprised—the most difficult place to live for Christ is at home. That's where people know us thoroughly . . . every nasty habit, idiosyncrasy, and weakness. It's where our mistakes and foibles are magnified.

During our seven-month engagement, Gail and I got to know each other very well. The pressures of our impending marriage exposed all sorts of interesting personality and character traits. But after the wedding, I was shocked at what I learned—not about Gail, but about myself. I didn't know that I could be so hateful and caustic, and that I would so willingly hurt the one to whom I had so recently pledged my undying devotion and love.

Marriage . . . family . . . the home can bring out the worst in us.

But if we're going to live for Christ *anywhere,* we have to live for him there. Home should be the first place that we apply the Bible, allowing God's Word to make a difference in our lives. The exciting truth, of course, is that the Bible has the answers to *all* of life, including family life. God can make a difference where we live, at home.

There are two main ways to find applications for home and family: (1) through the window of our lives, (2) through the window of the Word.

THE WINDOW OF OUR LIVES

The easiest way to begin the process of applying the Bible to our families is to start with ourselves—our daily problems and pressures, stresses and strains. By analyzing what we're going through, we can discover specific areas that need special attention. Then we can search the Scriptures for answers and applications.

Homestyle Categories

At first, we may not be able to pinpoint areas of need, except to remember specific, unpleasant incidents such as an argument with a son over curfew or frustration over a daughter's choice of friends. But every aspect of our lives at home should be considered. Also, specific incidents may be symptoms of a deeper problem.

To take a close look at our homes, we should think through each of our important family relationships. Here are some general categories to start us thinking: husbands and wives, parents and children, parents and teenagers, children and parents, extended family, the family together, adults at home, marriage, roommates.

We can make this even more specific by thinking through possible pressure points in those categories that apply to us. For example "husbands and wives" could cover love, friendship, sex, conflicts, communication, partnership, commitment, changes, pressures, leadership, in-laws, faithfulness, and others.

Home is also important for those who are unmarried. For a single adult living with a roommate, the areas to consider include conflicts, communication, privacy, partnership, friendship, and so forth.

"Parents and children" would include nurturing, communication, discipline, conflicts, training, goals, development, and others.

The idea is to look at Scripture through the window of our lives. To use another analogy, think of a doctor: he or she must first determine where we are hurting before prescribing the appropriate medicine.

Let's look at a couple of familiar Bible stories to see how this works.

Suppose you are studying Luke 18:18-30, the story of the rich young ruler. You determine that one of the principles being taught in this story is that nothing must come between a person and his or her relationship with God and that Christians should be willing to give up anything that competes with God for first place in our lives. While this story is not a direct teaching about the family, that principle can be applied in the home. Looking at the passage through your homelife-window, you may see that your relationship with your fiancée (or spouse) has become more important to you than God. Convicted by the Holy Spirit, you see that you should yield that relationship to Christ.

Or consider the love chapter, 1 Corinthians 13. The timeless truths contained in those profound thirteen verses apply to just about every facet of homelife. As you read this chapter thinking about your family, many applications will come to mind. Let me remind you of what I have mentioned several times previously in this book: It is not enough to determine a general application such as, "I should be more loving at home." Each application should be specific and tied to an action plan. You could say, for example, "Because love is patient, I should be more patient with my husband. Therefore, *if* he says something that usually irritates, *then* I will not respond with anger in my voice. Instead, I will listen patiently and wait to speak. And then I will speak gently and kindly."

And just think of the family applications of Jesus washing the disciples' feet (John 13:1-17), Paul's teaching on humility (Philippians 2:1-11), and James's discussion of the power of the tongue (James 3:1-12).

It helps to think of our pressure points and areas of need as we approach Scripture. These categories and specific areas will drive us to the Bible; and then the Bible will drive us back to our families.

Application Areas
Another way to discover how the Bible applies to us and to our homes is to think through the following general areas of personal application. Each of these categories covers innumerable specific family situations. I have included a few examples in each area.

1. *Relationships.* This would include any combination of relationships among husband, wife, children, grandparents, friends, other relatives, etc.
● Your aging father keeps making demands on your time.
● Your son has been arguing with you a lot lately.
● Your husband seems distant.
What relationship needs a special touch from God?

2. *Conflicts.* All relationships have conflicts, but there may also be internal, personal struggles. Both would fall under this category.
● You had a major blowup with your wife last night.
● You and your brother are at odds about whether or not to put Mom in a nursing home.
● The kids seem to fight over everything.
What conflict should be resolved? Where is a peacemaker needed?

3. *Personal Burdens.* Fears, dreams, hopes, goals, pressures, and other hidden thoughts and feelings are included here.
● Your eldest child is entering junior high and you're scared to death.
● You have been offered a terrific promotion at work, but it would mean moving to another state.
● You are struggling with self-doubts.
What burden needs to be lifted?

4. *Difficult Situations.* Spending money, correcting problems, communicating effectively, and disciplining children are a few of the tensions we can face at home.
● Your youngest child has been very stubborn and has started throwing tantrums.
● You have been following the government's example of deficit spending, and now the family finances are a mess.
● Your daughter has been suspended for fighting in school.
What problem must be solved or tension resolved?

5. *Character Weaknesses.* This area covers everything from lying to lust, and can refer to you or to any other family member.
● You discovered a stack of *Playboy* magazines under your teenage son's bed.
● You have been drinking more than usual lately.
● You are convinced that your brother has been lying to you.
Whom do you need to confront in love, and where do you need forgiveness and strength?

6. *Lack of Resources.* The three main resource areas are time, money, and abilities. Your family or individual family members may be struggling with deficits in these or other areas.
● Everyone is so busy that seldom is the whole family together during the week.
● Your wife has been promoted at work, but she's not sure she can do the job.
● The cost of living is rising faster than your paycheck.

What do you need?

7. *Responsibilities.* In addition to individual tasks and assignments, this category also covers how we carry out our responsibilities, including integrity, initiative, and industry.
● You have been asked to join the Principal's Parent Council at the high school.
● Your daughter was elected treasurer of her junior high student council.
● You teach an adult Sunday school class at church.
What do you have to do and how are you going to do it?

8. *Opportunities.* Homes are filled with opportunities to grow, learn, love, serve, and live for Christ.
● You want your kids to bring their friends to your house.
● A neighbor has been asking spiritual questions lately.
● The church is looking for families who will host ministry interns this summer.
How can God work though you in your home?

Clearly, just thinking about each of these areas will surface many needs and possible places for applying God's Word.

As you study the Bible, keep these homestyle categories and application areas in mind. They will provide many possibilities for homeward Bible applications.

THE WINDOW OF THE WORD
Another way to find biblical principles that apply to marriage and family is to begin with the Bible itself, studying those passages that deal directly with the home. Use the Pyramid (chapters 4 and 5) or the Application Window (chapters 6 and 7) as you study one of these Bible passages on marriage, home, and family.

Specific Teachings

Many passages dive right into the subject. Here are a few:

- Genesis 2:18-24—*achieving oneness in marriage.* While studying these verses, newly married Jason knew that he had to focus more on his bride and emotionally "leave home."
- Exodus 20:12, 14—*God's laws governing marriage and family.* During a study of the Ten Commandments, Brett was hit by the high value God placed on marriage and family. He knew that he had to rearrange his priorities.
- Exodus 34:7—*sin's consequences passed on through the generations.* When Gretchen heard this verse, she was struck by the far-reaching effects of her actions as a parent. She decided to remove a sinful habit from her life.
- Deuteronomy 6:4-8—*the importance of teaching biblical truth at home.* As he read this passage, Todd became convicted about the place of the Bible and church in his family. Even though his children were very young, he decided to initiate family times of Bible reading and prayer three times a week, at dinner.
- Matthew 19:3-12—*the intended permanence of marriage.* Sheila and Ben had been married for nearly twenty years, but they were hit by the force of Jesus' words about marriage in this chapter. They decided to renew their wedding vows, recommitting themselves to each other and to God.
- 1 Corinthians 7:1-16—*Paul's teaching on marriage in a lust-filled culture.* Cathi is a Christian, but her husband, Grant, isn't. As she read this passage at the women's Bible study, she became convinced of her responsibility to be a witness for Christ to Grant through her life and to stop telling others of his lack of faith.
- Ephesians 5:21-33—*submission and unity in marriage.* Frank had insisted on being the "head" of his house. But as he read this passage, he became convicted about his failure to love his wife "as Christ loved the church" (NIV).
- Ephesians 6:1-4—*special words to husbands, wives, parents,*

and children. When she heard these verses explained in family devotions, eight-year-old Tammy decided to be more obedient to her mom and dad. Her father decided to stop nagging the children, and he asked them to forgive him.

● 1 Timothy 3:4-5; 5:8—*the importance of caring for our families.* When Gregg and Marti read 1 Timothy 5:8, they knew they had to bring Gregg's elderly mother home to live with them.

A Bible concordance or topical study will lead you to other passages.

Proverbs

For wise advice that is right to the point, read the book of Proverbs. It's loaded with references to family life: fathers and sons (for example, 4:1-6; 5:1-21; 6:20-24; 20:7; 28:7), wives (for example, 12:4; 14:1; 18:22; 27:15), and parenting (for example, 22:6; 22:15; 23:13-14; 29:17). God also gives instructions concerning sex, fornication, and adultery. And there is the classic description of a truly good wife in 31:10-31.

Of course, a specific proverb doesn't have to be labeled "family" to apply. I have to remember Proverbs 15:1 daily. "A gentle answer turns away wrath, but harsh words cause quarrels." In fact, almost all of the proverbs can be applied to a family setting (even the principles behind those dealing with the kings).

Proverbs is a gold mine of applications for the home.

Examples of Families

We can also find home applications by looking closely at the family relationships described in the Bible. Whether a good example or a bad one, there are lessons to be learned and applied. Consider the interaction among Abraham, Sarah, Hagar, Isaac, and Ishmael. And then there's Rebekah's home, with Isaac, Jacob, and Esau. And look at the family dynamics at work with Joseph and his brothers.

Invaluable lessons can be gleaned from many other family situations: Ruth and Naomi, Eli and his sons, David and his wives and children, Hosea, Jesus and his earthly family, and Paul. Each situation provides an example to follow or avoid, a lesson to learn, and a principle to apply.

Putting faith into practice must begin where you live. You can find applications by looking at Scripture through your life experiences or by looking at your life through Scripture. In either case, for applying the Bible, *there's no place like home!*

WORKING IT THROUGH

1. Choose one of the Homestyle Categories (husbands and wives, parents and children, parents and teenagers, children and parents, extended family, the family together, adults at home, marriage, roommates) and use it to help analyze your family. List one or two problems, needs, challenges, or areas of concern that come to mind.

_____

What biblical principles relate to those situations?

_____

_____

_____

What might God be telling you to do about them?

_____

_____

_____

2. Choose one of the Application Areas (relationships, conflicts, personal burdens, difficult situations, character weaknesses, lack of resources, responsibilities, opportunities) and use it to help you think

through your relationships at home. List one or two specific problems, needs, challenges, or areas of concern that come to mind.

_____

_____

What biblical principles relate to those situations?

_____

_____

_____

What might God be telling you to do about them?

_____

_____

_____

3. Choose one of the following passages: Genesis 2:18-24; Deuteronomy 6:4-8; 1 Corinthians 7:1-16; Ephesians 6:1-4. List the biblical principles that apply to your family situation.

_____

_____

_____

Chapter at a Glance

Homestyle Categories:
- Husbands and wives
- Parents and children
- Parents and teenagers
- Children and parents
- Extended family
- The family together
- Adults at home
- Marriage
- Roommates

Application Areas:
- Relationships
- Conflicts
- Personal burdens
- Difficult situations
- Character weaknesses
- Lack of resources
- Responsibilities
- Opportunities

CHAPTER TWELVE
Pass It On

There are two types of people in the world: those who divide the world into two types and those who don't.

At the risk of sounding as silly as that statement, I want to divide the Christian world into two types of people: those who find Bible application easy and those who don't. If you are in the first category, then you probably have breezed through this book, especially the "Working It Through" sections at the end of the chapters. And if you're like many people I know, you think that everyone else is like you; in other words, you assume that others also can step easily from biblical principles to personal application.

"Wrong, hermeneutic breath!" The fact is that *most* people have difficulty seeing possible applications. For them, that "easy step" is a tremendous leap. If you are in this second category, right now you are probably nodding your head in agreement. You know what I mean. You have had to read this book slowly, thinking and working through each chapter—you have had to *learn* how to apply the Bible.

A popular psychological tool these days is the Myers-Briggs Type Indicator (MBTI). One of the categories in this tool is "Intuition" versus "Sensing." Intuitive people tend to operate with a sixth sense, seeing beyond the apparent to what could be in a given situation and imagining future possibilities. There is much more that could be said about people who think intuitively, but the important point here is that intuitive people tend to be in the group for whom Bible application seems to come naturally. But intuitive people are only about 30 percent of the population. As you might imagine, many pastors and Bible teachers are in this group. Often these preachers and teachers assume that everyone in their congregations or classes has that same application ability, so they fail to preach with application or to teach others how to apply the Bible. It's hard for them to understand how application can be difficult.

I like computers. A few years ago, I overcame "computer-phobia" and bought one—it has been a tremendous tool for me. But although I use a computer daily for my writing and editing work, I really don't know very much about computer science. So you know what drives me crazy? Computer experts who assume that I know what they're talking about when they use words such as *megabyte, ROM, DOS, Windows,* and so forth. Because it's their area of expertise (either computer literacy came easy for them or they worked hard to understand these marvelous machines), they assume that I am tracking with them at their level of understanding.

Before I get too holier-than-thou, however, I must admit that I often react the same way to those who find it difficult to do what I find easy. Take writing, for example. When I worked for Youth for Christ, I would send a monthly report to the financial supporters of my ministry. It would take me about an hour to write the letter, from planning what I wanted to say to handing it to my secretary. I made the mistake of assuming that everyone else on staff could do that as quickly as I could. I learned, however, that some staff members took hours and hours to write their letters. They weren't inferior, just different.

So don't assume that people know how to apply the Bible, even if they talk about application. Most need to be carefully taught. And because you have read this far, you know some techniques that others do not. So you can teach others—you can pass it on.

ASKING THE RIGHT QUESTIONS
When we wrote the notes for the *Life Application Bible,* we defined application as "confronting people with the right questions and then

motivating them to action." That's where teaching the application process begins. Whether you are a pastor or parishioner, teacher or student, leader or layman, you can ask the right questions.

In their simplest form, these questions are "So what?" and "Now what?"

A few years ago, I led an adult Sunday school class. I didn't have to do much preparing or teaching because we used a set of video-tapes by a well-known Bible professor. The topic was the book of Hebrews. Each Sunday I would turn on the TV and the VCR, put in the tape, and push the button. That was easy enough. Then we would sit, watch, and listen to this interesting and informative teacher. The class seemed to be learning a lot about Hebrews. And after each presentation, everyone was eager to discuss what we were learning. But I felt as though something was missing. Then I realized what it was: we weren't making the lessons personal; we weren't making any applications.

After thinking it through, I decided to change the class format. We still watched the tape first, with Bibles open as we followed along. Then afterward I would ask, "What new insight or piece of information did you learn today?" As class members shared, I would write their answers on the board. Next I would simply ask: "So what? In other words, what difference do those new insights, fresh ideas, and biblical truths make to *you,* in your life?" Suddenly Hebrews started coming alive as we discovered its relevance for us. Then I would end each class by asking, "Now what? What are you going to do about your answers to the 'So what?' question?" And I would allow time for everyone to write out their answers and design a plan of action. Our Sunday school class moved beyond the typical factual and informative, but impersonal, format.

Later, I shared that experience with the leader of a weekly Bible study for women. The next Sunday, she rushed up to me after the worship service and thanked me for my "tip." She explained that when she added the question "So what?" to her study, the women wouldn't stop talking. They came up with all sorts of answers and suggestions for application. They really began to apply the Bible lesson to their lives.

That's the place to start in "passing it on" to others. Ask the right question—"So what?"—and motivate to action—"Now what?" You can do this in your family devotions, a small group study, or a class, even if you're not the teacher or preacher.

TEACHING HOW TO APPLY
Next, you can teach others all the steps in studying and applying the Bible. This is important because it trains people to dig into God's Word for themselves—they don't have to depend on a spiritual leader for their growth. If you are a pastor, elder, Sunday school teacher, or small group leader, you have a ready-made forum for doing this.

In this book I have presented two Bible study methods, the Pyramid and the Application Window. I have found that the Pyramid is easier to teach to a group of people from a variety of backgrounds and personalities and with varying amounts of Bible knowledge. The Application Window has proven to be extremely helpful for personal study for some people and for pastors in their sermon preparation. So, for teaching groups of people how to apply the Bible, I recommend the Pyramid.

SUNDAY SCHOOL CLASS
Because the Pyramid has nine steps (*People, Place, Plot, Point, Principles, Present, Parallels, Priorities, Plan*), you could make this a nine-week topic for an adult Sunday school class. Of course you could teach more than one step some weeks and cover it in less time (for example, you could combine *People, Place,* and *Point*).

Be sure to give the class the atmosphere of a workshop or Bible study. In other words, don't spend the hour lecturing. Instead, each Sunday, after reviewing the past lessons and teaching the next step, allow time for everyone to work through at least two passages of Scripture. Remember, practice makes perfect.

SMALL GROUP

The same format would work well in a small group. Here you have the added benefit of meeting together for more than a quarter of the year. So after working through the Pyramid, you could put into practice what you learned by studying a book of the Bible together. Begin with a small book such as James, Mark, Philippians, or 1 John so that you can finish the book before the end of the year. Study a chapter or a section a week, rotating leaders so that everyone has the chance to lead others through the steps.

Another advantage of the small group is accountability. If the group is close, each week members can share their personal applications and action plans. Then at the next meeting, they can report on what they did to put the Bible lesson into practice.

SEMINAR

"How to Understand and Apply the Bible" would be an excellent topic for a special, one-day seminar. This could take place on a Saturday at the church. You could charge a nominal fee which would cover the cost of this book and lunch. (Did you get the hint? Give everyone a copy of this book!)

At the conclusion of the seminar, challenge participants to share what they learned with at least one other person (for example: spouse, child, Christian coworker or neighbor, ministry team member, etc.).

TEACHING YOUNG PEOPLE

It's never too early to learn that the Bible is God's Word and that it applies to life. Even with young children, we should be asking what they think they should *do* about what they have learned in Bible stories.

You can begin to teach young people how to study the Bible as early as junior high. It's important, however, to teach to their level of understanding, so don't hit them with the whole Pyramid. Instead, use a scaled-down version.

When I worked with Youth for Christ, I helped develop a five-step version of the Pyramid for junior highers using the steps *People, Plot, Point, Present,* and *Plan.* This is explained in detail in *Campus Life/JV, Year 1,* "How to Understand the Bible" (published by Youth for Christ/USA and available from YFC Sales, P.O. Box 228822, Denver, CO 80222). It is also presented in my book *Reaching Kids Before High School* (Victor Books), which you can order through a local Christian bookstore.

Here's a brief summary of the steps:

1. *People.* Identify the people in the story.
2. *Plot.* Answer "Who?" "Where?" and "What?" Put the story in your own words.
3. *Point.* Find the lesson or moral of the story (answering "What is God like?" or "What should people be like?")
4. *Present.* See how the point of the story relates to your family, friends, faith, or future.
5. *Plan.* Design an action plan for putting the point of the story into practice—by praying, looking, and doing.

These steps should also work well with high school students.

Someone has said: "You can feed a hungry man by giving him a fish. But you can feed him for a lifetime by teaching him *how to* fish." Help your brothers and sisters in Christ feed themselves *spiritually*—teach them how to understand and apply God's Word.

WORKING IT THROUGH

1. With whom can you share the Bible study Pyramid?

_____

2. In what group or class are you involved where you can introduce the questions "So what?" and "Now what?"

_____

3. What three steps can you take for teaching a class or small group, or for organizing a seminar, on applying the Bible?

a. _____

b. _____

c. _____

4. What can you do to teach children and young people about Bible application?

_____

_____

_____

CHAPTER THIRTEEN

Just Do It!

One of the more interesting experiences of my life is volunteer coaching for junior high girls. I say "interesting" because with that age group, every practice is an adventure. I never know what will distract them from listening to me and following my instructions at practice. Perhaps the most maddening characteristic is the attitude that they already know what I'm going to tell them.

Cheri stands at the free throw line. She aims carefully and launches the ball toward the hoop . . . but it doesn't come close. And she steps over the line in the process. "Cheri," I start to say, "stand with your feet a little farther apart, bend your knees, put your top hand here and your bottom hand here, start the ball down here, and then push—"

Before I can finish, Cheri answers, "I know," and proceeds to heave the ball awkwardly toward the rim again, missing the shot even farther than before.

Cheri may have heard my instructions (that was not the first time I had given them). And she actually *may know* how to shoot a free throw, as she stated so confidently. But even if she knows it, she isn't doing it. She isn't putting her knowledge into practice.

There's a big difference between *knowing* and *doing*.

But let's take this story a step further. Suppose I am a brilliant teacher of basketball skills, and soon every girl on my team can shoot free throws with deadly accuracy. Then I play a game on Saturday, but I don't come close on *my* free throws. In many ways, I'm no better than Cheri.

There's a big difference between *teaching* and *doing*.

If you have read this book and haven't skipped ahead to this chapter and if my writing has been clear to you, you should know much about studying, understanding, and, especially, applying the Bible. In fact, you may know the Pyramid and Application Window so well that you can teach them to your Sunday school class, small group, or seminar with ease. But remember, there's a difference between *knowing* and *doing,* and there's a difference between *teaching* and *doing.*

So as you conclude this book, ask yourself, Am I *doing* what God wants me to do? Am I obeying him?

Be honest in your self-evaluation:

● Where is God speaking to me?
● What areas of my life does he want me to change?
● What does God want me to *do* about what I have read in his Word?

Applying the Bible begins *now,* with *you.*
Just do it!

And remember, it is a message to obey, not just to listen to. "So don't fool yourselves. For if a person just listens and doesn't obey, he is like a man looking at his face in a mirror; as soon as he walks away, he can't see himself anymore or remember what he looks like. But if anyone keeps looking steadily into God's law for free men, he will not only remember it but he will do what it says, and God will greatly bless him in everything he does" (James 1:22-25).

APPENDIXES

Three Ways to Find Applications for Your Class or Congregation

Whether you are teaching a class or preaching topically or expositionally, you should know the needs of your people. Thinking through their real and potential needs will help you prepare applications for your teaching or sermons that really hit home.

NEED CATEGORIES

Needs may be categorized in many ways. For example, you could divide them into *felt* needs, *real* needs, and *spiritual* needs.

As the adjective suggests, *felt* needs relate to what people are feeling. These include physical and social pressures that they may be experiencing, so those needs are at the front of their awareness. Hunger is a felt need. So are loneliness, fear, and guilt.

Real needs are needs that people have but aren't aware of at the moment. An engaged couple should know about conflict resolution, for example, but usually they won't be feeling that need before the wedding. Other topics in the *real* needs category include communication skills, money management, and skills for living.

The third category is *spiritual* needs. Of course, any of the needs in the first two categories could fit in this one because "spiritual" is not limited to a specific area or compartment of life. But "spiritual needs" are the special demands of God on life and the implications of what it means to call Christ Lord. Involvement in church, sharing the faith with others, studying the Bible regularly, and praying about everything are examples of topics in the *spiritual* needs category.

APPLICATION AREAS
Another way to surface your congregation's needs is to think through the eight areas of personal application (discussed in chapter 11). These areas are:
1. Relationships (family, friends, neighbors, coworkers, fellow believers)
2. Conflicts (in marriage, with children, at work, in the neighborhood)
3. Personal Burdens (sickness, family pressures, death, loss, etc.)
4. Difficult Situations (stress, debt, hindrances, etc.)
5. Character Weaknesses (integrity, image, lust, selfishness, etc.)
6. Lack of Resources (time, energy, money, materials, abilities, information)
7. Responsibilities (work demands, church programs, volunteer efforts, home projects, etc.)
8. Opportunities (learning, working, serving, etc.)
   As you read this list while thinking of your people, the Holy Spirit may show you a real need in your class or congregation. Or you could refer to this list as you study the lesson or Sunday's text.

DAILY OBSERVATIONS
A third way to locate application areas is to look for them as you relate with people and observe the world. Needs may surface during pastoral calling, hospital visitation, after-service conversations, counseling appointments, youth work, board and committee meetings, newspaper reading, and during a typical day at home or on the job. When you look for ways to apply the Bible to life, you will find them.

APPENDIX B
Application Techniques

Here are some simple techniques to use in personal Bible study and application.

● *Explanation, Bridge, Application.* This is the formula used in writing the notes for the *Life Application Bible. Explanation* explains what the text says. *Bridge* shows how the biblical principle is relevant today. *Application* challenges the reader to take action. This is also a good structure for a short devotional.

● *Role-play Bible People.* Put yourself in the shoes of each person in the Bible story to see what he or she must have been feeling and thinking. Consider how you would react if you were him or her in that situation.

● *Apply to Others.* Think of someone who really needs to learn the lesson of the passage you are studying. Then consider how you are similar to that person.

● *Intensify the Need.* Think of a need in your life and imagine it to be much worse than it is. Then think of God's timeless truths that apply to that need. Those truths probably apply to your less intense need as well. Many times we don't make the connection because our needs aren't serious; intensifying the need can help us see the application.

● *Put It in Writing.* Whenever you make a personal application, write it down in a Bible study notebook, diary, or journal. This will help you focus your thoughts, help hold you accountable, and give you a good indication when you look back of how God has been working in your life. Even if you don't ordinarily keep or file away these diaries, writing down your thoughts can help you spot applications.

● *S P I E S.* Think through the problems, pressures, and deficits in your life using these categories: Social, Physical, Intellectual, Emotional, Spiritual.

● *F F F F F.* Use these categories when screening your life for places to apply Scripture: Family, Friends, Future, Fears, Faith.

● *Use Analogy.* Think of an example from another area of life that will illustrate the application point. For example: Trying to live the Christian life without reading the Bible is like trying to shingle a roof without a hammer and nails, trying to fish without a pole or a net, trying to play golf without clubs . . . it won't work.

● *"Watch me . . ."* To see if you've understood the lesson or sermon and to see if the application is relevant and concrete, complete this sentence with what you think you should do: "Hey, teacher (or preacher), watch me _____."

● *Look at the Other Side.* Look at the lesson or application from the opposite perspective. Ask, "How might this *not* work?"

● *Look from God's Perspective.* As you read, ask, "Why did God put this in the Bible?"

● *Make a Joke.* When finding applications seems difficult, take a humor break. Imagine the people in the story laughing; look for humor in the story; make a joke.

● *Action Lab.* Give yourself an assignment that you will fulfill before the next study.

● *Zingers.* Think of short punch lines in the passage that you could use in a conversation. Then use them on yourself.

● *Reverse.* Read the teaching or story as if it had the opposite meaning. For example, Matthew 6:2 states: "When you give a gift to a beggar, don't shout about it as the hypocrites do—blowing trumpets in the synagogues and streets to call attention to their acts of charity!" You could change this to read, "When you give a gift to a beggar, shout about it. . . ." Noting the practical or character problems that would result from this reverse teaching can help you see more clearly what the Bible is saying.

Questions and Answers

Question: In a Bible study group, how can I, as the leader, get people into the text?

Answer: Use an icebreaker activity or several interesting and non-threatening discussion questions that foreshadow the application (or touch on the topic you will discuss). These openers should start with real life experiences, paralleling the application in a neutral area of your group's experience. We must start where people are or they will never connect with the text. For example, you could have a quiz on current events, ask questions about television shows, hold a mini scavenger hunt for items that people have with them, construct hypothetical moral dilemmas and ask what the characters should do, etc. These openers should create interest in the text or the topic.

Question: Sometimes we get bogged down early in our Bible study and never get to application. What can I do to keep the discussion focused and moving?

Answer: The easiest way is to appoint a timekeeper. The three main steps in Bible study are *Observe, Interpret,* and *Apply.* Decide beforehand how much time to spend on each step. For example, if you decide to spend an equal amount on each, in an hour study you would spend twenty minutes at each step. If you use the Pyramid, consider taking 25 percent of your time on the first three steps as you climb the Pyramid (*People, Place, Plot*), 25 percent on the next two steps (*Point, Principles*), and 50 percent on the last four steps as you descend (*Present, Parallels, Priorities, Plan*). Have the timekeeper keep the group on track, and don't allow questions to move back to the previous steps.

Another solution to this problem is to suggest applications at every step instead of saving them until the end (when time is limited and everyone is thinking about the refreshments or leaving).

Question: As I lead a Bible study, how can I be concrete without being threatening?

Answer: The best way is to write and then read case studies, typical situations in which people who are similar to your group members find themselves. You could describe a family situation where the parents are having a tough time with their teenager, a potentially compromising situation at work, a struggle to make ends meet financially, interpersonal conflicts, etc. Then ask what the featured person in the story should do; how he or she should respond. You should ask, "What biblical principles apply to this situation?" And you could even ask, "What would *you* do in this situation?"

Question: How do the *Life Application Bible Studies* follow the Pyramid?

Answer: The five sections in each lesson of a *Life Application Bible Study* are *Reflect, Read, Realize, Respond,* and *Resolve. Reflect* is an opening question to get the individual or group thinking about the topic and preparing them for application. *Read* looks at the text itself and would be parallel to the *People, Place,* and *Plot* steps in the Pyramid. In *Realize* we look for the timeless truths in the passage—*Point* and *Principles* on the Pyramid. *Respond* answers the question "So what?" and covers the *Present, Parallels,* and *Priorities* steps in the Pyramid. Finally, *Resolve* answers "Now what?" as does *Plan* in the Pyramid.

Question: How can I motivate my Bible study group, and myself, to follow through on our applications?

Answer: Establish accountability links among the group. This can be the group as a whole—when you meet, you check with individuals about whether or not they followed through from the last meeting. But it is probably more effective in pairs or partners—two people who covenant to pray for each other and keep each other on track in their Bible study and applications.

Question: What are some other helpful resources for application-oriented Bible study?

Answer: As you might expect, I highly recommend any of the Bibles and books in the Life Application line from Tyndale House Publishers. These include:

● *Life Application Bible*. Currently available in the New International Version, *The Living Bible,* the King James Version, and the New Revised Standard Version; the complete text of the Bible with more than ten thousand notes and many other helpful features such as Megathemes, outlines, Personality Profiles, cross-references, maps, and an index to application topics.

● *Life Application Commentary Series*. A fresh, new commentary on the entire Bible (to be released in sixteen volumes), focusing on application.

● *Life Application Bible Studies*. Each study contains the complete text of the *Life Application Bible* for the book of the Bible being studied and thirteen lessons for studying that book; the entire New Testament and several books of the Old Testament are available in the New International Version; many books are available in *The Living Bible*.

● *Handbook of Bible Application*. Notes from the *Life Application Bible* arranged by topic to help teachers, speakers, and pastors.

● *Life Application Bible for Students*. A terrific Bible for junior high and senior high young people; loaded with helpful notes, including Moral Dilemma Notes, "Here's What I Did" notes, Ultimate Issue Notes, Application Notes, a Life-Changer Index, a Bible Reading Plan, "I Wonder" notes, Personality Profiles, a Follow Through Course for New Christians, highlighted Memory Verses, and much more.

Here are a few additional resources that are strong in application.

● GroupBuilder Resources (Victor Books)—new discussion books for adult small groups, focusing on relevant topics and centered on Scripture.

● Shaw Contemporary Issues Series (Harold Shaw Publishers)— study guides for individual or group use; each study addresses an important contemporary issue from a biblical perspective (for example, ambition, leadership, priorities); eight studies in each book.

● Small Group Study Series (Victor Books)—each book has six sessions for youth and young adults; centered around felt needs of youth (for example, identity, dating, sex, leadership).

● *Small Group Ministry with Youth* by David R. Veerman (Victor Books)—invaluable help on starting small groups, understanding group dynamics, leading a discussion, and more; highlights several small group ministry models.

● *Effective Bible Teaching* by James Wilhoit and Leland Ryken (Baker Book House)—an excellent and practical resource for Bible teachers; includes helpful information for personal Bible study as well.

● "The 50-Day Spiritual Adventure" with Chapel of the Air Ministries—studies, books, sermons, and other materials for the whole church; loaded with application.

● *Taking the Guesswork Out of Applying the Bible* by Jack Kuhatschek (InterVarsity Press)—good summary of the principles of application; helpful section of specific types of application.

Apply Each Type of Bible Literature*

TYPE: **Law**	**Books:** Genesis, Exodus, Leviticus, Numbers, Deuteronomy
PURPOSE	*Civil Law:* to help Israel organize, mobilize, and survive as a nation.
	Ceremonial Law: to govern Israel's worship, with specific instructions for the tabernacle, temple, sacrifices, and offerings.
	Moral Law: to give God's rules for life. These rules transcend culture and time.
WHAT TO LOOK FOR	*Principles behind the Laws* Example: "If anyone makes a rash vow, whether the vow is good or bad, when he realizes what a foolish vow he has taken, he is guilty" (Leviticus 5:4). The principle is that we should be wise and self-controlled, not promising what we cannot do or what would be wrong to do.

*This chart originally appeared in *Discipleship Journal* 58, 59 (1990).

Personal Examples to Follow or Avoid
Korah (see Numbers 16) is an example of someone with many significant abilities, but whose
ambition caused him to lose everything.

*Israel's Development Paralleling Our
Spiritual Growth*
We know from 1 Corinthians 10:1-11 that what
happened to Israel occurred as examples and
warnings for us.

HOW TO APPLY

Principles
The principles are timeless, so look for contemporary and personal applications.
Example of an application (Leviticus 5:4):
When someone asks if I can do something, I
shouldn't make a foolish promise, exaggerating
my ability to perform.

Personal Examples
Look for people or situations that you can identify with—parallels in your life.
Example of an application (Korah): I must
guard against ambition and greed.

Israel's Development
Put yourself, your church, or your country in
Israel's place in the story. Look for similar situations today.
Example of an application: During the wilderness wanderings, the nation of Israel grumbled
constantly, failed to trust God, and slipped into
idolatry. I shouldn't repeat these mistakes when
facing my own "wilderness" experiences.

| TYPE: **History** | *Books:* Joshua, Judges, Ruth, 1 Samuel, 2 Samuel, 1 Kings, 2 Kings, 1 Chronicles, 2 Chronicles, Ezra, Nehemiah, Esther, Acts |

| PURPOSE | To record facts about events and people, showing how God has worked in history. |

| WHAT TO LOOK FOR | *Negative Examples*
Example: Hophni and Phinehas (1 Samuel 2, 4) illustrate the results of greed and blatant disobedience. |

Positive Examples
Example: Nehemiah exemplifies godly and effective leadership.

Cycles of Sin and Obedience
Example: The book of Judges shows that during prosperity, the people of Israel would grow complacent and self-sufficient, eventually living totally apart from God. Then God would punish Israel by allowing them to be conquered by enemy nations. The people would respond by repenting and crying out to God for help. God would raise up a godly judge who would deliver Israel from her enemies. Then the people would remain loyal to God under the leadership of that judge, and the nation would prosper. But when the judge died, they would slip back into sin, and the cycle would begin again.

| HOW TO APPLY | *Negative Examples*
Avoid making the same mistakes. |

Example of an application (Hophni and Phinehas): God will punish deliberate sin. As a leader in my church, I should be careful to obey God and be sensitive to sin in my life.

Positive Examples
Copy the lifestyle of the godly person.
Example of an application (Nehemiah): In every phase of Nehemiah's leadership, his first step was to pray. To be an effective leader for Christ, first I must be a person of prayer.

Cycles of Sin and Obedience
Look for evidence of these cycles in your life, family, church, and nation.
Example of an application (Judges): God is blessing me with prosperity and things are going well, so I must guard against complacency, self-sufficiency, and pride.

TYPE: Poetry (Poems and Wisdom Literature)	*Books:* Job, Psalms, Proverbs, Ecclesiastes, Song of Solomon
PURPOSE	To express feelings to God and to give practical guidelines for living.
WHAT TO LOOK FOR	*Practical Wisdom* (especially Proverbs and Ecclesiastes) Example: Proverbs tells about people who have wisdom and enjoy its benefits. A proverb is a short, wise, easy-to-learn saying that calls a per-

son to action. It doesn't argue about basic spiritual and moral beliefs, but assumes that we already hold them. Proverbs are not "laws," or moral absolutes. Rather they are catchy statements that express practical truisms. Proverbs 14:7 says, "If you are looking for advice, stay away from fools."

Worship (expressions of praise and adoration for God)
Example: "O Lord our God, the majesty and glory of your name fills all the earth and overflows the heavens. You have taught the little children to praise you perfectly. May their example shame and silence your enemies!" (Psalm 8:1-2).

Attributes of God (descriptions of what God is like)
Example: Job 38–41 gives a fresh and powerful description of God's majesty and might.

HOW TO APPLY *Practical Wisdom*
Take each statement as a personal, common-sense directive.
Example of an application (Proverbs 14:7): I must weigh carefully anything I hear from that neighbor who is always acting and talking foolishly. His advice will probably not be good.

Worship
Use the psalmist's expressions as examples of how to pray and worship, opening yourself up to God.
Example of an application (Psalm 8:1-2): Every

day I should thank God for his majesty, power, glory, and goodness.

Attributes of God
Look for God's attributes and respond accordingly with a new appreciation for who God is. Example of an application (Job 38–41): I shouldn't doubt or question God for what I am going through and what he is doing in my life. Instead, I must humbly trust myself to him, knowing that he knows and wants what is best for me.

TYPE: Prophecy

Books: Isaiah, Jeremiah, Lamentations, Ezekiel, Daniel, Hosea, Joel, Amos, Obadiah, Jonah, Micah, Nahum, Habakkuk, Zephaniah, Haggai, Zechariah, Malachi

---

PURPOSE

Prophets (along with priests) were God's special representatives. The purpose of their prophecies, therefore, was to confront national leaders and the people with God's commands and promises. In doing this, often they would also foretell the future.

WHAT TO LOOK FOR

The Prophet's Role (seeing how he lived)
Example: Ezekiel had to endure tremendous hardships in order to faithfully present God's messages (Ezekiel 4, 12, 24).

The Character of God (seeing God in action as he relates to the prophets and studying the prophets' pronouncements)
Example: When Isaiah was commissioned, he

had an overwhelming sense of God's holiness
and his own sinfulness (Isaiah 6).

Social Action (references to specific social conditions)
Example: "I will not leave them unpunished any
more. For they have perverted justice by accepting bribes and sold into slavery the poor who
can't repay their debts; they trade them for a
pair of shoes. They trample the poor in the dust
and kick aside the meek" (Amos 2:6-7).

HOW TO APPLY

The Prophet's Role
Put yourself in the prophet's place and ask what
message God wants you to give.
Example of an application (Ezekiel): I must be
willing to do whatever it takes to tell others
about Christ, even if it means looking foolish in
front of my friends.

The Character of God
Look for what God's actions and messages
reveal about his nature.
Example of an application (Isaiah): My sinfulness becomes very apparent in light of God's
holiness; therefore, I must confess my sins and
submit myself to his leadership.

Social Action
Look for similar social conditions in our world.
Example of an application (Amos): I must
oppose politicians, business people, and others
who oppress the poor, and I should become
involved in working with the poor in my community.

TYPE: **Gospels** (Biographies of Jesus)	*Books:* Matthew, Mark, Luke, and John
PURPOSE	To give an accurate record of Christ's birth, lifestyle, teachings, death, and resurrection
WHAT TO LOOK FOR	*Jesus' Lifestyle* Example: Jesus often showed compassion on the sick and dying, even touching lepers as he healed them (Mark 1:40-45).
	Ethical Teachings (specific statements about how people, especially Jesus' followers, were to live) Example: In the upper room, Jesus said, "And so I am giving a new commandment to you now—love each other just as much as I love you. Your strong love for each other will prove to the world that you are my disciples" (John 13:34-35).
	Parables (stories with a message) Example: Luke 8:4-15 presents the parable of the four soils.
	Figures of Speech (word pictures that Jesus used to describe himself and his kingdom) Example: Jesus described the kingdom of heaven as a pearl of great value (Matthew 13:45-46). (Note: the categories for "History" also apply here)

HOW TO APPLY *Jesus' Lifestyle*
Jesus said that if we want to know what God is
like, we can look at him (John 14:9), and Paul
wrote that the goal of the Christian life is to be
like Christ (Romans 8:29). Therefore, we should
model our lives after Christ.
Example of an application (Mark 1:40-45):
Jesus touched lepers, the "AIDS victims" of his
day. I should have compassion on those who are
hurting and do what I can to relieve their suffering.

Ethical Teachings
Jesus' ethical statements are timeless, so look
for where they hit you.
Example of an application (John 13:34-35):
I must be loving to my Christian brothers and
sisters, even when I don't feel like it or when
they irritate me.

Parables
Consider Jesus' interpretation of the parable and
the context to discover the timeless truth. Then
bring that principle into a current situation.
Example of an application (Luke 8:4-15): In
which areas of my life am I good soil (open to
God's Word)? In which areas am I hard, rocky,
or thorny? I must work to make all the areas
"good soil."

Figures of Speech
Put yourself in the story. Ask: "How is Christ
'bread' (or water, etc.) to me?"
Example of an application (Matthew 13:45-46):
The kingdom of heaven is invaluable—nothing

else in life compares. I must make it the number one priority in my life.

TYPE: Epistles

Book: Romans, 1 Corinthians, 2 Corinthians, Galatians, Ephesians, Philippians, Colossians, 1 Thessalonians, 2 Thessalonians, 1 Timothy, 2 Timothy, Titus, Philemon, Hebrews, James, 1 Peter, 2 Peter, 1 John, 2 John, 3 John, Jude

---

PURPOSE

To give Christians and churches doctrine and principles for living

---

WHAT TO LOOK FOR

Doctrines
Example: In Galatians 3, Paul explains the relationship between law and faith.

Ethics (direct statements on how we should act)
Example: James 3:13-14 states that believers should be humble and not be bitter, jealous, or selfish.

Church Conflicts (often the occasion for writing an Epistle)
Example: In 1 Corinthians 6, Paul discusses the problem of believers taking each other to court.

HOW TO APPLY

Doctrines
You should have a solid theological foundation, knowing the facts of the faith. But then you should allow those truths to permeate your life. Doctrines will most often affect your attitudes first and then your actions.

Example of an application (Galatians 3):
Christ's death freed me from the law. So I
shouldn't put myself in "bondage" by trying to
earn God's favor by doing all the right things.
Instead, I should live by faith, daily depending
on God and allowing the Holy Spirit to work
through me.

Ethics

These straightforward statements about life
should be brought into contemporary settings
and obeyed.
Example of an application (James 3:13-14): I
must confess the bitterness I have over an incident in the past, letting it go and letting God
heal that relationship.

Church Conflicts

After understanding the culture and the conflict,
look for the relevant principle. Then you will be
able to apply that principle to similar situations
in your church. You can also learn from watching how Paul and other church leaders resolved
their conflicts.
Example of an application (1 Corinthians 6): If I
have a conflict with a fellow believer, I should
try to resolve the issue and not take it to court
(even though suing has become a way of life in
this country).

TYPE: **Apocalypse** *Book:* Revelation

PURPOSE

To give believers assurance and hope through a
God-given glimpse into the future

WHAT TO LOOK FOR	*The Church* Example: In Revelation 2:4, God's message to the church at Ephesus says, "Yet there is one thing wrong; you don't love me as at first!"

Hope
Example: In Revelation 22:12 we read, "See, I am coming soon, and my reward is with me, to repay everyone according to the deeds he has done."
Example: *Judgment and Victory*
Example: "I saw the dead, great and small, standing before God; and The Books were opened, including the Book of Life. And the dead were judged according to the things written in The Books, each according to the deeds he had done" (Revelation 20:12).

HOW TO APPLY *The Church*
The first three chapters are messages to specific first-century churches in Asia, but they are typical of churches and believers throughout the centuries. Reading God's messages to these churches can give you insight and direction in your church setting.
Example of an application (Revelation 2:4): Our church used to be on fire for God, but now we seem complacent. I should talk with the pastor about my concerns and see how I can be a catalyst for a spiritual awakening.

Hope
The first readers of this book were oppressed believers, many of whom were facing torture and death because of their faith. How are you in

a similar situation? How can this book give you hope?

Example of an application (Revelation 22:12): Although I feel almost overwhelmed by sorrow, I know that this life is not all there is. Christ will return and reunite me with Mom.

Judgment and Victory
Christ will be victorious, and all sins will be punished and wrongs made right. What implications do the events described in Revelation have for you?

Example of an application (Revelation 20:12): Although it often looks like evil is winning in this world, I should remember that Christ will triumph. This should motivate me to be faithful and to be prepared for Christ's return.

STEPS TO PEACE WITH GOD

1. **RECOGNIZE GOD'S PLAN—PEACE AND LIFE**

   The message you have read in this book stresses that God loves you and wants you to experience His peace and life.

   The BIBLE says . . . *"For God loved the world so much that He gave His only Son, so that everyone who believes in Him may not die but have eternal life." John 3:16*

2. **REALIZE OUR PROBLEM—SEPARATION**

   People choose to disobey God and go their own way. This results in separation from God.

   The BIBLE says . . . *"Everyone has sinned and is far away from God's saving presence." Romans 3:23*

3. **RESPOND TO GOD'S REMEDY—CROSS OF CHRIST**

   God sent His Son to bridge the gap. Christ did this by paying the penalty of our sins when He died on the cross and rose from the grave.

   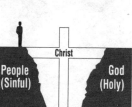

   The BIBLE says . . . *"But God has shown us how much He loves us—it was while we were still sinners that Christ died for us!" Romans 5:8*

4. **RECEIVE GOD'S SON—LORD AND SAVIOR**

   You cross the bridge into God's family when you ask Christ to come into your life.

   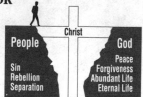

   The BIBLE says . . . *"Some, however, did receive Him and believed in Him; so He gave them the right to become God's children." John 1:12*

THE INVITATION IS TO:

REPENT (turn from your sins) and by faith RECEIVE Jesus Christ into your heart and life and follow Him in obedience as your Lord and Savior.

PRAYER OF COMMITMENT

"Lord Jesus, I know I am a sinner. I believe You died for my sins. Right now, I turn from my sins and open the door of my heart and life. I receive You as my personal Lord and Savior. Thank You for saving me now. Amen."

If you want further help in the decision you have made, write to:
Billy Graham Evangelistic Association, P.O. Box 779, Minneapolis, MN 55440-0779